CCCC STUDIES IN WRITING & RHETORIC

Edited by Victor Villanueva, Washington State University

The aim of the CCCC Studies in Writing & Rhetoric (SWR) Series is to influence how we think about language in action and especially how writing gets taught at the college level. The methods of studies vary from the critical to historical to linguistic to ethnographic, and their authors draw on work in various fields that inform composition—including rhetoric, communication, education, discourse analysis, psychology, cultural studies, and literature. Their focuses are similarly diverse—ranging from individual writers and teachers, to work on classrooms and communities and curricula, to analyses of the social, political, and material contexts of writing and its teaching.

SWR was one of the first scholarly book series to focus on the teaching of writing. It was established in 1980 by the Conference on College Composition and Communication (CCCC) in order to promote research in the emerging field of writing studies. As our field has grown, the research sponsored by SWR has continued to articulate the commitment of CCCC to supporting the work of writing teachers as reflective practitioners and intellectuals.

We are eager to identify influential work in writing and rhetoric as it emerges. We thus ask authors to send us project proposals that clearly situate their work in the field and show how they aim to redirect our ongoing conversations about writing and its teaching. Proposals should include an overview of the project, a brief annotated table of contents, and a sample chapter. They should not exceed 10,000 words.

To submit a proposal, please register as an author at www.editorial manager.com/nctebp. Once registered, follow the steps to submit a proposal (be sure to choose SWR Book Proposal from the drop-down list of article submission types).

D1590327

GENRE OF POWER

POLICE REPORT WRITERS AND READERS IN THE JUSTICE SYSTEM

Leslie Seawright
Missouri State University

Conference on
College Composition
and Communication

National Council of
Teachers of English

Staff Editor: Bonny Graham
Manuscript Editor: JAS Group
Series Editor: Victor Villanueva
Interior Design: Mary Rohrer
Cover Design: Mary Rohrer and Lynn Weckhorst

NCTE Stock Number: 18429; eStock Number: 18436
ISBN 978-0-8141-1842-9; eISBN 978-0-8141-1843-6

It is the policy of NCTE in its journals and other publications to provide a forum for the open discussion of ideas concerning the content and the teaching of English and the language arts. Publicity accorded to any particular point of view does not imply endorsement by the Executive Committee, the Board of Directors, or the membership at large, except in announcements of policy, where such endorsement is clearly specified.

NCTE provides equal employment opportunity (EEO) to all staff members and applicants for employment without regard to race, color, religion, sex, national origin, age, physical, mental or perceived handicap/disability, sexual orientation including gender identity or expression, ancestry, genetic information, marital status, military status, unfavorable discharge from military service, pregnancy, citizenship status, personal appearance, matriculation or political affiliation, or any other protected status under applicable federal, state, and local laws.

Every effort has been made to provide current URLs and email addresses, but because of the rapidly changing nature of the Web, some sites and addresses may no longer be accessible.

Library of Congress Cataloging-in-Publication Data

Names: Seawright, Leslie, author.
Title: Genre of power : police report writers and readers in the justice system / Leslie Seawright, Missouri State University.
Description: Urbana, Ill. : National Council of Teachers of English, [2017] | Series: Studies in writing & rhetoric | Includes bibliographical references and index.
Identifiers: LCCN 2017034852 (print) | LCCN 2017016258 (ebook) | ISBN 9780814118429 (pbk.) | ISBN 9780814118436 ()
Subjects: LCSH: Police reports—United States. | Police reports—Arkansas.
Classification: LCC HV7936.R53 S43 2017 (ebook) | LCC HV7936.R53 (print) | DDC 808.06/6363—dc23
LC record available at https://lccn.loc.gov/2017034852

For my favorite person on the planet, John Cameron Seawright.
May you inherit a world more caring and peaceful than I did.
Momma is trying. . . .

CONTENTS

ACKNOWLEDGMENTS

MANY BRILLIANT, KIND, AND THOUGHTFUL SCHOLARS, family members, and friends contributed to the creation of this book. I first thank the person who inspired and made most of this work possible, my husband, John Seawright. Though he is no longer a police officer, his entry into, work within, and exit from policing served as the catalyst for the research and writing of this book.

I thank my friend and mentor David Jolliffe, who helped shape the initial study in this book and guided me through my dissertation. He continues to be a constant source of support and encouragement. I will forever be grateful for Ellen Cushman, who tirelessly read each chapter of this manuscript. She would often cheer me on by saying, "Leslie, you are the only one who can write this book." Thank you. Cheryl Glenn and Becky Rickly provided support and advice, and taught me how smart, tenacious women succeed in the academy. Thank you for all you do to inspire and encourage female academics.

My friends and former colleagues at Texas A&M University at Qatar, Nancy Small, Mysti Rudd, and Amy Hodges, provided me with a source of strength that continues to inspire and renew me each day. My years spent in Qatar with these women will forever be one of the greatest experiences of my life. I love you all.

I am thankful for the advice and support of several Texas A&M University at Qatar guest speakers: Shirley Brice Heath, Sam Dragga, Deborah Brandt, Yvonne Lincoln, Marianne Cotugno, and Sam Wineburg. I must thank the generous administration at Texas A&M University at Qatar for providing summer research funds that allowed me to travel and conduct interviews with police officers and attorneys.

There are some truly generous and selfless members of my University of Arkansas cohort who have been there for me from the beginning. Eve Baldwin, Gamil Alamrani, Jake Edwards, and Jeannie Waller have demonstrated time after time what it means to be a friend and colleague. Thank you. At my current institution, Missouri State University, I must thank W. D. Blackmon and Rhonda Stanton for their support of this project and my academic career.

This book was created in part through the careful input and suggestions of SWR reviewers, the editing team led by Bonny Graham, and the series editor, Victor Villanueva. It was Victor's book *Bootstraps* that inspired me to write the book *I* wanted to write, one filled with story, autobiography, theory, and critique. I am grateful for the time and energy he put into making this manuscript what it is today.

Finally, I would like to express my sincere gratitude to the anonymous officers, attorneys, judges, and individuals featured in this book. Thank you for the time, experiences, and thoughts you shared with me. It is my greatest hope that together we can build communities that respect and value all members.

INTRODUCTION

"All we have right now is what's in the police reports, which is nothing. When I see those police reports, they tell me, 'Hear no evil, see no evil, speak no evil.'" (Justin Bamberg, lawyer representing the family of Walter Scott, qtd. in Fernandez)[1]

POLICE OFFICERS WIELD A GREAT DEAL OF POWER IN THE United States. Human and civil rights hang in the balance based on their observations, decisions, and documents. People go to jail. People don't go to jail. Justice is served. Justice is not served. Police are heroes. Police are villains. How police officers wield their power and through what mechanisms are critical questions for scholars to answer. Several important philosophers and theorists have critiqued police practice and the institutions of State power.[2] These discussions continue to filter down into composition and rhetoric, technical writing, and workplace writing studies to aid in the study of genre, agency, power, and social systems. Although police interviewing practices have been studied in good detail (Rock; Edwards; Haworth; Stokoe and Edwards; Kidwell and Martinez; Komter), fewer researchers probe the ways in which police writing, and specifically the police report, is taught and works in the system. (Campbell; Cotugno and Hoffman; Miller and Pomerenke).

"BAD" POLICE REPORTS

Prior to my research efforts at the Jackson Police Department,[3] I had always heard that police couldn't write; police reports were worthless documents; no one should ever trust what a cop wrote down. It was also well known in my academic and social circles that police reports were not allowed in court because of how poorly they were written (a misperception). My initial research into police writing revealed similar sentiments. Prosecutors, police chiefs, defense attorneys, and even officers complained to me about how poorly police reports are written. I heard this sentiment expressed in casual conversations as well as in formal interviews with police chiefs, prosecutors, and defense attorneys. The mountain of texts dedicated to improving officer report-writing skills demonstrates the problems associated with report writing. Titles such as *How to Really Really Write Those Boring Police Reports* (Clark), *Plain English for Cops* (Meier and Adams), *Painless Police Report Writing* (Frazee and Davis), and my favorite, *The Best Police Report Writing Book with Samples: Written for Police by Police, This Is Not an English Lesson* (Michael), say a lot about how reports are viewed by officers and superiors. Report writing is seen as boring, difficult, convoluted, painful, and overly concerned with grammar. The manuals' typical solutions are templates and simplified demands to include the who, what, when, where, how, and why of every encounter. They largely avoid the context of police writing as a rhetorical situation fraught with complicated audience needs and multiple, often conflicting, purposes.

It became clear to me after reviewing police academy materials and sitting in on two different report-writing training sessions that report writing was taught from a deficit model. Police cadets were instructed on how to write a coherent paragraph and use the correct word for a specific meaning. They were also instructed on how to organize the report, detailing the events chronologically. However, the majority of the police academy training I researched was spent on ground-fighting tactics, shooting practice, crime scene investigation, and multiple-choice test preparation. At the police academy in Arkansas, only 8 hours out of 430 were devoted to report writing (Seawright).

When I asked officers, lawyers, supervisors, and others what made a police report a "poor report," the answers varied wildly. Officers seemed to think that poor grammar created poor reports. Supervisors and chiefs complained about a lack of professionalism in reports. Stephen Mathes, the police chief of the Jackson Police Department, complained that "basic grammar" just wasn't present in police reports. He noted,

We are not just taking a raw recruit and trying to teach them law and police tactics but basic grammar in some instances. . . . [I]f a defense attorney picked up a report that was poorly written they are automatically going to say, here is a person I can attack. I can attack credibility.

However, the lawyers I spoke with complained that their most serious concern regarding police reports was the amount of information that was often left out. Two hours after my interview with the Jackson police chief, I sat in the office of Chad Rucker, a local defense attorney, who stressed the importance of the police officer narrative over grammar in report writing. He emphasized, "Only in telling the story can all the details of the case come to light. Grammar does not matter. It could be written phonetically for all I care, just put down everything that happened."

So within a matter of hours, a police chief had told me that grammar really mattered to defense lawyers, and a defense lawyer had told me that he couldn't care less about grammar in reports. How was it that the police report genre could elicit such varied and contradictory expectations from its readers? These two men know one another. They have seen each other socially and even discussed cases from time to time, yet they have no comprehension of how differently they think about the content and form of a police report.

For the attorney, the content takes precedence over form because he is concerned about understanding the story of what took place; for the chief, the form in terms of grammar and professional presentation takes precedence. This difference in emphasis is just one of the struggles that officers must navigate when writing reports. The police report genre is critical because it links evidence, testimony, victims, suspects, and others in the legal system to one another and to the power of the institution or social system. This book tackles several questions regarding the police report genre. I explore what is at stake mainly in terms of cultural and social capital for police report writers and their readers. In addition, this text attempts to identify how the police report document accrues or loses power in the judicial system.

DISCOVERING POLICE WRITING PRACTICES

In order to understand the police report genre, its multiple readers and contexts, I conducted qualitative research over a period of six years. My methods included ethnographic field notes, interviews, observation, and discourse analysis. I spent more than 240 hours riding in police cars and going on calls with officers. In addition to hours of informal conversations with officers, I conducted formal interviews with eighteen police officers from multiple agencies in three different states. These officers included six police trainers, two supervisors, two chiefs, and one sheriff. In addition, I interviewed three prosecuting attorneys, two defense attorneys, and two judges. I reviewed thousands of pages of training manuals from three different departments. I reviewed forty hours of police training and police traffic stop video and personally observed the report-writing training class in two police academies. I read hundreds of police reports and many of the manuals that address police writing. In addition to my intensive study with the Jackson Police Department in Arkansas conducted over six years, I also conducted interviews and collected materials from a large urban city department in Oklahoma, a suburban department in Colorado, and two state university police departments. A grounded theory approach[4] best fit the environment and needs of this kind of study. I started collecting data and interviews prior to understanding the problems associated with report writing. As I continued to research the writing of police officers, more questions emerged. These questions led to more data collection and comparative analysis, and so developed the cycle of grounded theory research that started six years ago and continues today. My main findings reveal surprising conflicts between reader expectations, the ways in which a police report "works" in the system, and how power circulates in the hierarchical chain of police report readers.

For instructors and scholars in composition, rhetoric, and other fields, discovering how such documents accrue power and how readers use the same document for different purposes is important. Knowing an audience, whether addressed or invoked to use the categories made famous by Ede and Lunsford ("Audience Addressed";

"Among the Audience"), is not enough in many environments. Police officers know and interact with many of the readers who will read their documents, and also assume an invoked audience of potential jurors, media, and public citizens for their reports; yet in crafting their documents, officers are quick to ignore reader expectations that conflict with their own. Audience expectations and conflicts in power, genre, and a writer's need for self-preservation create writing environments vastly more complicated than the picture we sometimes present to students. To ignore the realities of complex writing situations with multiple and conflicting audience interests is to ignore the true contexts of many of the genres that we teach, such as the report, proposal, letter, memo, and others.

THE COMMUNITY

Jackson, Arkansas,[5] is a thriving city of around 55,000 people located between the green hills of northeastern Oklahoma and the stunning beauty of the Ozark Mountains. The population of Jackson is 62 percent white, 30 percent Latinx, and 2 percent African American. These racial demographics are similar to those of cities in the surrounding area. The Latinx population has increased dramatically over the past three decades, rising 137 percent from 2000 to 2010 alone.[6] There are several Latinx-owned grocery stores, restaurants, and other business in the area.

Jackson enjoys a robust economy thanks to three large Fortune 500 companies headquartered in the area. Because of the region's prosperity, residents of Jackson have a household median income 35 percent higher than the average for the state of Arkansas. Though the largest urban center is over 100 miles away, the smaller communities located in this section of Arkansas have a combined population of almost 350,000. A state university is located here, as is a community college and other regional colleges within commuting distance.

Jackson citizens enjoy a lively downtown area, recently renovated and renewed by the chamber of commerce, a golf course, several gated neighborhoods, an industrial area, and outdoor recreational areas. The town hosts several annual events including a Christmas parade, July 4th celebration, Halloween carnival, food festival, and numerous expositions held at regional convention centers. Situated between two main highways that run through Arkansas, the community enjoys easy commutes between towns, tourism opportunities, and a vibrant location.

The Jackson Police Department's new headquarters was recently constructed, and combines the call dispatch center, administration offices, records department, misdemeanor courtroom, holding jail cells, patrol room, and officer computer lab in a large building with an attractive façade. This new building is already at capacity in terms of available office space and multipurpose rooms. As the population of Jackson has continued to climb, so has the number of police officers and officials.

There are approximately 100 officers employed by the Jackson Police Department. The majority of officers are white males. At the time of my research, the only diversity in the department was provided by three Latinx male officers and two white female officers. Jackson police officers are hired in one of two ways: (1) as a recruit with little to no experience in law enforcement and no official certification, or (2) as a transferring police officer who is currently certified in Arkansas or another state. In the vast majority of cases, those hired have little to no prior experience in law enforcement. They are selected through a rigorous process that includes a background check, a psychological exam, a lie detector test, and interviews with a civil service panel, police officials, and the Jackson police chief. New employees are hired conditionally, based on their ability to complete police academy training and become certified officers in the State of Arkansas. Currently, there is no requirement for advanced degrees beyond a GED or high school diploma. Recruits must be twenty-one years old and have no felonies on their records.

The academy is located in Arkansas and includes recruits from several community police departments in the area. Classes are taught by officers from various departments in Arkansas who volunteer to teach a class or two each term. Once a recruit from the Jackson Police Department completes academy training, he or she is placed with a training officer who serves as a mentor for the following three months. During this period, the recruit learns the specific procedures of the Jackson Police Department and becomes introduced to the culture and customs of the department.

The chain of command at the Jackson Police Department, as in most departments, is a critical component of the system. Officers report to one of four shift supervisors who are at the rank of sergeant. This group of sergeants, along with other sergeants representing specific units such as SWAT or criminal investigations, report to one of two lieutenants who both report directly to the chief. Maintaining the chain of command in communication and reporting is expected of every new recruit and veteran officer. In this model, the Jackson PD is paramilitary in its structure, as are most police departments in the United States.

CHAINED LITERACY EVENT

Heath's concept of the literacy event serves as a useful tool when looking at police report readers. Heath first identified the concept after observing women in a community working together to create meaning while reviewing, reading, and discussing a letter from the school district. She notes that the women "bring in knowledge related to the text and interpret beyond the text for their own context; in so doing, they achieve a new synthesis of information" (*Ways* 201). The reading of a text could not be separated from the previous knowledge, experiences, and beliefs the women held individually and collectively. Likewise, police reports are read, examined, critiqued, defended, refuted, and discussed by multiple audience members in multiple settings. Each individual brings his or her own context and knowledge to the interpretation of the text. Some of this meaning making is done by the reader on his or her own, and sometimes it is done with others, in court for example. The readers of the report form a chain whereby they read the report in a specific and hierarchal order.

The first to read the report after the officer has written it is the supervisor. He or she examines the document prior to its final submission, a responsibility that supervisors hold for all the reports from officers on their specific shifts. Next, the document goes to the prosecutor, who must decide based on the information in the report whether to file charges against the suspect(s) implicated in the report. If charges are filed, the report moves to a defense attorney (private or public), who will be tasked in finding a way to defend the client. If the case moves to trial, the report may, at a certain point, come under the scrutiny of a judge. Though the judge may not read the actual report, because these are only rarely allowed as evidence, a police officer will be asked to testify. When officers testify in court, they almost always rely on their written police reports to refresh their memories of the events. Thus, the judge will hear and be able to act upon a report as it is used in court. As a result of their decisions, the readers are all linked to what is in the written document and linked by the hierarchy of the justice system and the order in which the report is read. As the report moves along the hierarchical chain of readers, linking and tying their decisions to one another, a chained literacy event is created.

The journey of the police report from one reader to the next constitutes a type of literacy event, but other literacy events reside in each link of the chain. Although the officer is responsible for writing the report based on his or her observations, I have observed officers often relying on one another for guidance in report writing. At the Jackson Police Department, many officers use the computer lab to write their reports at the ends of their shifts. When in the lab, officers ask questions of one another, search for the correct term, suggest proper charges, and offer support to the other report writers. When several officers have been on the same call, they will often review the call together and help the lead officer write the report. This collaborative writing effort includes reading and referring to other documents, such as state statute books, dictionaries, online forms, and policy and procedure manuals. A literacy event emerges even in the first stage of the police report's chained literacy event.

Although the review of the report is often done solely by the supervisor on duty, he or she may review other materials or ask a lieutenant to read the document in order to determine what changes the reporting officer should make in the report. If the supervisor decides that the officer needs to make revisions, these suggested changes are written and communicated back to the officer. The officer then takes these written suggestions for revision, interprets them, and incorporates the changes (or not) into the report for the final submission.

Once the prosecutor's office receives the report, it is read and a decision is made about whether to file the charges recommended by the arresting officer. The prosecutor may or may not agree that probable cause has been met for the recommended charges. He or she may not believe there is enough evidence to take the suspect to trial, even though the initial arrest is legal and the officer had probable cause in making an arrest. For court, a prosecutor must meet a higher burden of proof than probable cause. The prosecutor's job in the initial reading of every report is to determine if, in fact, the officer had probable cause for the arrest and if there is enough evidence to file all or some of the charges in the report. When the facts in a case are unclear, a prosecutor may decide to null process all but the most apparent violation of the law.

A defense attorney works with his or her client, the prosecutor, and witnesses to review the details in the report and construct a defense. The attorney may highlight certain parts of the report in order to persuade the prosecutor to accept a lower charge and create a plea deal for a client. In reviewing the report, a client may offer new information an officer did not include in the report or refute details the officer did include. Witnesses, interviewed by the defense attorney and questioned about the police report, may offer additional information that changes the understanding of the event documented in the report.

Finally, in court, all these people come together to utilize or refute the police officer's documentation of the events and arrest. The multiple meanings and readings of the document must be considered by the judge and a verdict given. The chained literacy event is thus made up of small but powerful literacy events occurring at every link in the chain.

THE POLICE REPORT GENRE

The police report is a genre that documents the observations of a police officer within a legal context. The genre is created by officers but used by many. It is intended to serve the community's interests by protecting citizens through the prosecution of lawbreakers. Few studies in rhetoric look specifically at the police report as a genre, despite the fact that scholars and the public at large are generally interested in the workings of police operations and organizations. Devitt claims, "Studies of particular genres and of particular genre sets . . . can reveal a great deal about the communities which construct and use those genres, and studies of particular texts within those genres can reveal a great deal about the choices writers make" ("Generalizing" 581). This book seeks to do just that. By following one text in the police report genre, I hope to reveal insights into the practices and beliefs of the police community. In addition, I hope to raise important questions about the police report genre and its complicated position between the officer and the court. Paré, for example, questions the fairness of genres to the parties involved and impacted by them (139–41).

It is critical that a study of the police report genre focus not only on the writer and the text, but also on how police reports are read and by whom. Bazerman argues that a genre "provides a writer with a way of formulating responses in certain circumstances and a reader a way of reorganizing the kinds of message being transmitted" (62). Genres shape not only the writer in the act of writing, but also the reader in the act of reading. Bawarshi, in agreement with Bazerman, claims that genres build context as much as they are within contexts. Genres "help us function within particular situations at the same time they help shape the ways we come to know these situations. Genre reproduces the activity by providing individuals with the conventions for enacting it" (340). In terms of activity and contexts, Bawarshi argues that "genres are social constructed cognitive and rhetorical concepts—symbiotically maintained rhetorical ecosystems if you will—within which communicants enact and reproduce specific situations, relations, and identities" (352).

In the following chapters, one police report document will be examined as representative of the larger genre of police reports. The contexts that shape report writing as well as those contexts that *are created* by the writing will be considered.[7]

THE MATTER OF RACE

During the writing of this book, Michael Brown, Tamir Rice, Eric Garner, Walter Scott, Freddie Gray, Sandra Bland, and many others became symbols for police brutality and systemic racism. While Baltimore, Maryland, and Ferguson, Missouri, were burning, citizens across the United States took to social media and the streets to protest the loss of what many deemed innocent lives. Even President Barack Obama noted during the riots in Baltimore, "We have seen too many instances of what appears to be police officers interacting with individuals, primarily African-American, often poor, in ways that raise troubling questions. This has been a slow-rolling crisis. This has been going on for a long time. This is not new, and we shouldn't pretend that it's new." (qtd. in Davis and Apuzzo). President Obama expressed the frustration that many Americans share regarding race relations and police power in the country. However, while slogans like "Black Lives Matter" could be found on everything from t-shirts to Facebook profiles, a counter movement was quickly established. "All Lives Matter" and "Police Lives Matter" soon became rallying cries of the Right and police supporters. America found herself divided again in matters of police or state power and individual rights, protections, and freedoms.

These incidents are not unique in US history, nor is the public outcry that followed them. In 1992, Los Angeles burned for days after the Rodney King trial verdict in which four white officers were found not guilty in using excessive force during the beating of unarmed King (*LA Times* Staff). This level of violence against people of color and the subsequent protection of officers (often white) has become systematic in many places in America. Bonilla-Silva, citing several different studies, concludes that "blacks and dark-skinned Latinos are the targets of racial profiling by the police, which, combined with the highly racialized criminal court system, guarantees their over-representation among those arrested, prosecuted, and incarcerated" (2).

Bonilla-Silva blames this over-representation on the practice of how black or minority areas are patrolled. When police officers focus on and only patrol minority communities, they begin to see minorities as criminals (49–50). This belief may be a working part of their subconscious and may affect black and Latinx officers as easily as it affects their white coworkers. Of course, the system in which the officers work may be more to blame, as it incentivizes arrests and incarcerations over community building and engagement. So, when an officer sees his or her job as making arrests and getting the bad guys, and this officer mainly patrols minority communities, he or she begins to see these places as rife with crime and minorities as criminals. The system feeds itself, and the stereotype becomes a fixed bias.

Despite efforts in the last century to rectify institutional and systemic racism, civil rights laws, rather than overturning decades of prejudice and discrimination, have actually reinforced whites' economic and social positions in society. The reason behind this is that whites fought fair housing acts, school desegregation efforts, and fair hiring laws so ferociously that the resulting legislation was often ineffective and unenforceable (Lipsitz 24–27). Even laws that seemingly have nothing to do with race, like Stand Your Ground laws, end up impacting minorities. The tragic fatal shooting of Trayvon Martin in 2012 is perhaps the most well-known example of the past few years, in which an innocent and unarmed African American youth was shot and killed by a civilian neighborhood vigilante. The Stand Your Ground law in Florida at the time of the shooting allowed citizens to shoot someone in self-defense even if retreat was an option. In 2014, rather than repeal the law that let Martin's killer, George Zimmerman, go free, Florida lawmakers sought to make the law broader by allowing "warning shots" (Strassmann).

Many people claim to be color-blind when it comes to race, and I have heard many in law enforcement claim the same. There are problems with this view. Radcliffe notes that "many well-meaning people promote gender-blindness and color-blindness as 'solutions' to the 'problems' of gender and racial differences[;] . . . these blindnesses mostly reinforce the status quo" (134). Because we whites live in a white world, it is often difficult to see how the environment privileges our actions and ambitions.

Frankenberg interviewed dozens of white women in her study of race and feminism. She found that many of the women attempted to gloss over, downplay, or disregard the very real racial problems in their own communities and lives. She finds that despite our efforts to claim that racism doesn't affect us or people we know, "racism shapes white people's lives and identities in a way that is inseparable from other facets of daily life" (6). Facets, then, such as the day-to-day working life of a white police officer. This is important to my study because all of the people I interviewed and the subjects of the police report are white (and nearly all are male). In such a scenario, it would be easy to ignore race in the analysis, but because racism is part of the system that we live within, it is important to discuss it in terms of power and policing even when its role doesn't seem immediately obvious. Mills reminds us, "The fish does not see the water, and whites do not see the racial nature of a white polity because it is natural to them, the element in which they move" (76).

This book records interviews with white male officers, attorneys, and judges. Their perspectives represent in many ways what it means to be white, male, and powerful in our society. Mills reminds us that the present reality of white dominance is "no longer constitutionally and juridically enshrined but rather a matter of social, political, cultural, and economic privilege based on the legacy of conquest" (73). I don't want this book to be another attempt by a white writer to neglect completely the issues of race that lie beneath our entire society. Although this book's primary focus is not on critical race theory, it is impossible to write about police and the justice system without including discussions of race and power.

CIRCULATING POWER AMONG REPORT
READERS AND WRITERS

Winsor argues that "the generation of power through discourse should be examined . . . texts play a role in the way in which power is created and deployed" (11). This study specifically examines the ways in which readers use police reports for their own purposes and how these readers gain, lose, or redistribute various types of capital in the process. I demonstrate that a police report's position of power—and that of its writer—is determined by individual readers and their own authority or agent position within the larger system and context. Different systems and contexts affect or change the power the document holds for each reader. The position, status, and capital of the writer are at the mercy of various readers and their own interpretations of the text.

I use three categories of capital developed by Bourdieu to aid the discussion of power, the police report genre, and the chained literacy event. Bourdieu first used the idea of cultural capital in order to explain the social inequity he saw in education ("The Forms"). The concept of cultural capital has evolved over time to mean the knowledge, possessions, and traits that a person acquires while being part of a particular group, organization, or class. Cultural capital in this study will refer to accumulated skills and knowledge, not just facts but the knowledge of systems, patterns, and how things are accomplished in certain settings.

Social capital is described by Bourdieu as the "basis of the existence of the group . . . in the hands of a single agent or a small group of agents [who] . . . exercise a power incommensurate with the agent's personal contribution" ("The Forms" 251). He gives the example of a father, the head of the household, who is the only one authorized to speak for a family. In this text, I use social capital as the reputation, status, stature, or prestige of an individual or group.

Finally, understanding symbolic capital is key to understanding how institutions remain in control and recreate themselves. Bourdieu claims symbolic capital is "that invisible power which can be exercised only with the complicity of those who do not want to know that they are subject to it or even that they themselves exercise it" (*Language* 164). Symbolic power is the control that people, organizations, or systems exert over their environments and over others. The subtle nature of this form of power, "invisible" as Bourdieu calls it, masks the agents who control it. This concept will be critical in understanding how police report writers and readers come by means of power that affect the legal system and society. Each chapter in this book will look at how the different forms of capital and power I have outlined here circulate forward and backward to readers of the police report.

OVERVIEW

Police reports can deeply impact people's lives and the system that is supposed to protect all of us. Their significance cannot be underestimated, and yet it remains that so little is understood about their writers and readers, contexts and constraints, power and purposes. As the quotation that opened this chapter reminds us, if a report says "nothing," and if officers choose not to or are persuaded away from revealing all the facts and circumstances of an event, then justice cannot prevail. The aim of this book is to investigate how officers create these vital documents and how these documents are then interpreted by various readers. Essential to this investigation will be determining how the genre of police reports operates and how power accrues and circulates in the chain of readers. This discussion will include the topic of race and how the men I interviewed demand and distribute power through the police report genre.

While this book only closely examines the path of one police report, my interviews with report readers offer many ways in which these findings can be generalized more broadly. Many of the lawyers noted how similar the report that I showed them was to the ones they read daily. Thus, I believe that the findings from this one in-depth case study, taken together with the hours of ethnographic and interview research I have done outside of the study, allow for greater generalizability than the findings from this one report alone.

The first chapter introduces Officer Lewis, the writer of the report used for this study. I take you to the scene of the domestic violence disturbance and then back to the police department computer lab as Officer Lewis creates the report based on his observations. Each chapter that follows offers a portrait of a police report reader as he works to identify important information in the report and use it in ways that best serve his purposes. It will be clear early on that each reader is doing something very different with this report and for very distinct purposes. The conflict between readers and writer will become apparent as interviews along the hierarchical chain are revealed.

In each chapter I discuss how the specific reader uses the document, how this use enables or constrains his own social capital, and in what way the police report genre is (re)creating the institution through symbolic power. Micro-chapters are also presented throughout the book. These short narratives offer glimpses into an officer's experiences on the job. The narratives are intended to build on the qualitative data offered here, presenting a multifaceted picture of what it means to be an officer in day-to-day practice.

Micro-Chapter

The Fire

I WAS ASLEEP IN THE PASSENGER SEAT OF THE PATROL car when my husband, Officer John Seawright, ran out of the building. It was 4:00 a.m., and I awoke to see him and several other officers running toward their cars in the Jackson Police Department parking lot. As I tried to orient myself to my location and situation, my husband threw the car into reverse, and we sped toward the lot exit.

"What's going on?" I managed to get out as we raced to some unknown location.

"Fire," he said. "Big one."

We turned onto a quiet residential street, and I could smell the smoke. One block down, a house was completely engulfed in flames. Red and orange gas blew out from the roof. On the lawn, a woman in her nightgown sat on the grass, her hair smoldering. My husband parked in the middle of road and started sprinting toward the woman. Only he and one other officer had made it to the scene so far. The fire trucks would be another three to five minutes away because the firefighters had surely been sleeping, like me, and would have to dress, grab their gear, and leave the station traveling at a much slower speed than my husband's patrol car.

Though I could not leave the safety of the police car, I was still intimately informed about what was going on outside. All police officers at Jackson are outfitted with lapel microphones in order to record their police stops. These systems automatically begin recording whenever the patrol car goes over a certain speed or has the lights and siren activated. Inside the car, my husband's microphone was revealing the conversations and events as they happened in real time.

He hurried to the woman sitting on the lawn. She screamed, "My husband is inside the house!"

The two officers turned and ran toward the burning structure. As they stood on the front porch, orange flames poured out of the windows and front door within a few feet of them. They shouted to one another, "It's too hot! Go to the window! IT'S TOO HOT! We gotta get in there! I can't get near the door! Go to the window! The fire is too hot! Where is he? It's too hot! Can you see anything? Oh, man! I can't see! It's too hot!"

I heard my husband gasp for air, and the telltale signs of an unavoidable asthma attack began.

I screamed inside the police car in complete panic, "Don't go in the house! Get away from the house!" I was horrified and helpless as I sat hearing my husband attempt to enter the home while his lungs shut down. Where were the fire trucks? Where were the other police cars? I desperately tried to understand why my husband, with no oxygen, no gear, and no protection, was attempting to enter a house entirely engulfed in flames. "Don't go in the house!" I screamed again.

"Where is he? It's so hot! We gotta get outa here! Come on, come on! We gotta get out! Go! Now! Go!" John and the other officer backed away from the front door of the house, afraid they would be overcome by smoke and heat. They raced to the back of the house and jumped the three-foot chain-link fence. There, in the backyard and ten feet from the house, they found an elderly man in his pajamas facedown in the grass. He had made it out of the house, but had collapsed and succumbed to smoke inhalation. The officers looked at him and, immediately realizing he was dead, turned their attention back to the woman on the lawn. They raced back to the front of the house, where I could see the woman smoking a cigarette. As the smoke rose, I couldn't tell where the smoke from the cigarette ended and the smoke from her charred hair began.

"Ma'am, ma'am, are you okay?" my husband asked her.

"Yeah, I think so," she replied. "You find him?" Fire truck sirens were getting closer to our location. I heard them first over the radio as they were picked up by John's lapel mic, and then seconds later on my own. The reflection of red and blue lights now danced above me on the patrol car roof.

"Yes, ma'am. We found him," John replied.

She looked down at the grass, said "Good," and took a long drag from her cigarette.

My understanding of police work changed dramatically the night of the fire. I had observed drunk-driving calls, domestic violence disturbances, car wrecks, breaking-and-entering scares, robberies, missing children reports, mundane music disturbances, and speeding stops; however, nothing prepared me for watching my husband, without any protective gear, try to enter a house that was fully engulfed in fire. His role as a police officer, and what that role asked of him, was already complex without the addition of the complete disregard for his personal safety. It was the reality of his role as a police officer that I didn't fully understand until I was forced to watch him do it.

My position as a police officer's wife and as a composition and rhetoric scholar allowed me to appreciate criticism of the police while engaging with the realities of policing and the real people who wore the uniform. My positioning as wife and scholar provided me the ability to research in both an etic and an emic position.[1] I am grateful for the access I had to those who work in the justice system, and I am likewise thankful to the scholars who aided my critique of that system.

1

Writing for Institutional Memory and Self-Preservation

> Institutions are embodied in part by bricks and mortar, and money, and printed forms, and policies, and the people that uphold them. . . . Reinforced by the resources and rules that guide behavior, those practices constantly reproduce the system, which is maintained through regulations which are in turn reinforced by sanctions or rewards.
>
> —Blyth 177

IT WAS A WARM THURSDAY EVENING IN JACKSON, ARKANSAS. I was riding with Officer Kale Lewis, a relatively young officer who had been employed by the Jackson Police Department for a little over one year. He had graduated with a degree in business from a state university but entered police work shortly after graduation. His police training was paid for by the Jackson PD, and his training was within the guidelines of the Arkansas Law Enforcement Training Academy, Arkansas Commission on Law Enforcement Standards and Training, and the Jackson Police Department Field Training Program. I had not met Officer Lewis prior to this night, but he was kind and quick to welcome me.

One hour into our eight-hour shift (11:00 p.m.), the Jackson PD dispatcher sent Officer Lewis and me to an address where a domestic dispute was underway. Prior to our arrival at the home, we knew the call to Jackson 911 had come from a person not involved in the altercation but who was inside the home; one or more of the parties may have been intoxicated; the caller refused to stay on the line because she was afraid she would be physically injured by the man involved in the altercation; there were no known weapons in the home. Officer Lewis turned on the police lights and quickly made his way to a neighborhood only a few streets from our location. We arrived at a small one-story house in a neighborhood of homes built in the 1950s and 1960s. The neighborhood and home showed obvious signs of poverty. As a resident of Jackson, I knew that this was a less prosperous area of town. A woman in sweatpants and a t-shirt was standing in the doorway of the house. Two police cars pulled up behind us mere seconds after we had parked the patrol car. The three officers, including Officer Lewis, exited their vehicles and walked cautiously up to the house. While I was instructed to remain in the car for my own safety, Lewis turned on his lapel microphone so that I could hear him and those around him while he was out of the car and interviewing witnesses. The mic audio was linked to an in-car audio/video system that records events and allows them to be used for evidence. I relied on this audio information, Officer Lewis's story, and the other officers' comments regarding what happened inside the home.

The officers had difficulty determining who was at fault after questioning the four people in the home (two white women and two white men). The female witness, who met the officers at the door, claimed she had heard the other woman in the house screaming, "Don't hit me. Don't hit me" during the incident. The male witness declined to comment at all. The two suspects had very different stories about what had happened and who had started the altercation. The suspects were asked by Officer Lewis to write out a description of what had happened that evening. They were provided with generic Jackson PD witness statement forms, which they filled out after being interviewed by the officers. Both the man and the woman involved argued in interviews and in their written statements that they had been unfairly attacked without provocation. Ultimately, both were handcuffed, arrested, and put in separate cars for transport to the county jail. The woman was very upset about being arrested. She tried desperately to explain to officers that she was not at fault and threatened to have her lawyer file charges against them.

The female suspect had bruising on her back and had been hit in the head. The male suspect had been sprayed in the face with wasp spray but had no other injuries. At the scene, the officers agreed that the best thing to do was arrest both the man and the woman for domestic violence. In the State of Arkansas, as in many other states, the decision to arrest someone for domestic violence is no longer left up to the victim. Domestic violence is now a crime against the State, and this allows police officers on the scene to determine who is at fault. The change in the law was meant to empower victims who were too afraid to "press charges" against their partners, children, or other household members.

Two officers drove away with the man and woman in separate cars and headed for the county jail, an inconvenient forty-five-minute round trip, while Officer Lewis and I headed back to the Jackson PD to write up the report.

REPORT-WRITING CONSTRAINTS

The fleet of police vehicles at Jackson Police Department are outfitted with onboard laptop computers, direct-link Internet, GPS, and complicated panels that control the lights, radio, public address system, and other important functions. Officers who work during the day are encouraged to log onto the Jackson PD database and create reports in their cars, but officers who must write reports at night almost always choose to do so back at the Jackson PD building.[1]

Officer Lewis entered his access code on a panel outside the back door of the police station around 12:30 a.m., and we entered the building. It was quiet inside, and only half of the hallway lights were illuminated. We walked past the patrol room, where officers meet before each shift for a briefing from their supervisors, and into the Jackson PD computer room. A desk-height counter ran the length of the two longest walls. On one side were three computers spaced evenly along the counter. On the other side of the room, there were only two. A black ergonomic desk chair was placed in front of each computer. The monitors on the counters were the large console type, not the sleek flat screens that are the more current and popular choice. A bookcase placed near the entry door held paper forms, blank witness statements, and other materials. Several volumes of Arkansas legal statutes along with dictionaries were lined up on one section of the long counter. In the corner of the room was a large printer, and above it a poster describing how to recognize false identification cards. On this poster and other parts of the wall were taped cartoons featuring police officers, notices on new procedures from supervisors, copies of newspaper articles, and other miscellany.

I sat down next to Officer Lewis as he pulled out his notebook and the suspects' written witness statements in order to begin writing the report from the domestic violence call. While every officer is required to submit his or her narrative of what occurred on scene, Jackson PD also has an integrated police report–writing database that asks officers to enter suspect names, witness names, addresses, and other pertinent information. In addition, there are several screens of check boxes, drop-down menus, and fill-in boxes addressing various details related to the crime that officers must fill in prior to writing the narrative.

Despite his short time as an officer, Lewis seemed confident in his writing and reporting skills. He commanded a good deal of knowledge about his own report-writing process. As he pulled up the Jackson PD database in order to begin the report, he confessed, "I graduated with a degree in business so, um, you know, I've had quite a few writing classes. But, you know, it can be a challenge for other people."

As Officer Lewis began filling in several check boxes in the system that would generate his report, I asked him who reads police reports.[2] He responded,

> Judges, attorneys, uh, me down the road if it does go to court. You want to be as detailed as possible, that way when you do get up there on the stand you can, you know, always have something to look back on, that way you're not caught saying something that is not necessarily a lie but, but, you know. If you're not detailed on them [reports] they can all just merge together.

Officer Lewis, while listing himself last as a potential reader, spends the rest of his response detailing the report as a device for his own use. He almost immediately jumps to the report's use as a mnemonic document for court. There is tension regarding the officer's perception of court, as he intimates that he doesn't want to be "caught saying something that is not necessarily a lie." He alludes to the fact that to be caught telling a lie (or something close to it) would result in a bad outcome for him in a court proceeding. There is a sense of fear here that remains unstated but present. The officer tries to explain that the details of various events can "merge together," making the report a critical document for him to keep track of events and insure his reputation in court. The report's purpose in this initial statement is mnemonic and instrumental. It records details for the user or writer to use again at a future date. At the same time, Officer Lewis gains social capital, which I define for the purpose of this study as status and reputation, through a report that makes him look like a qualified officer in court.

I asked Lewis about his strategy for organizing information in police reports. He explained that he has a simple outline that he uses for every police report. He includes the time, the location, the reason for the call, and what he observed on the scene when he first arrived. These details constitute the first paragraph of his police reports. After this information, he tries to explain each side of the story from each party's perspective in subsequent paragraphs. Lewis noted during our interview that he tells the story of one side, including any written witness or victim/suspect statements, and then tells the other side in the report. He makes the last paragraph of each report his conclusion. He mentioned that this outline was something that he created after working with different field training officers and reviewing their report organization. Jackson PD, unlike other departments, does not have specific requirements on how reports are organized by paragraph and where specific information should be included in the report. In other departments, reports are often written according to very detailed templates. One department in Oklahoma, for example, uses specific headings for each paragraph of a report and requires that certain information be included in each paragraph. Jackson PD allows for more freedom in how reports are organized and written, so Lewis created his own template to use for report writing.

As Lewis wrote "Domestic Battery 3rd Degree" in a blank on his report form, I asked him if he would purposely include the elements of the statute for Domestic Battery 3rd Degree in the report, or if he just assumed the prosecutor would look at the facts and make that determination. For every state, federal, and most local legal statutes, there are specific elements of each offense that must be met in order for a person to be charged with that crime. Lewis explained, "Well, you know, I don't have all the statutes in my head. A lot of times we have to refer to these [pointing to an Arkansas Legal Statute book]. Third Degree is basically no weapons were involved. Nobody was seriously injured." While he understands the main distinctions of Domestic Battery 3rd Degree, he seems unconcerned about justifying the charge in the report. He may assume that his audience is well aware of legal statutes and distinctions, perhaps even more so than himself. For this or other reasons, Officer Lewis does not seem concerned about including the specific legal language from the statute in his report.

I noticed Lewis struggle to explain the wasp spray as a weapon on the next report form drop-down menu. He was forced by the menu to select a specific description from several items provided under the heading "Weapon." The box required him to make a selection and constrained his ability to simply describe the item exactly (wasp spray). He finally decided on "Poison" but remarked, "A lot of times these [reports] get kicked back. And it's like, even if you do something that makes sense, they still get kicked back because they have a way that they want them." The report form forces Officer Lewis to describe the wasp spray as a "poison," even though he is clearly uncomfortable with that description. The complexity of each police call and the millions of variations possible from event to event make filling in even seemingly innocuous blanks a challenge in report writing.

Lewis also seemed frustrated because "even if you do something that makes sense," reports can get rejected. Once the report is submitted into the Jackson PD system, the supervisor will read it, comment on it if needed, and send it back to the officer for revision. Officer Lewis is talking about this process by which his reports come back to him for revision at the request of other higher-ranking officers. If, as it seems for Lewis, the report represents a memory of the event and is a valuable asset in court, the act of writing a report could be seen as one of self-preservation. Requests for alterations to the report from outside the writer may meet with resistance because they limit or change the officer's authority and agency.

Officers often find themselves, to use Herndl and Licona's term, in an act of "constrained agency" (134). Despite the fact that officers are in a position of authority when writing reports, fill-in-the-blank report forms, the report genre, supervisors, and other limitations constrain their writing. Police officers are not agents; rather, they are writers occupying positions of agency granted to them by specific social and cultural structures. Police officers write in positions of agency that are granted to them by the structures and systems within which they work and live.

Bourdieu claims that society is made up of many different social fields, for example politics, education, culture, and economy. Fields are occupied by individuals and institutions in hierarchal power structures. These people and institutions compete for resources, which Bourdieu calls capital (*Language* 171–201). Officers compete with the institution and with other officers for social and cultural capital. They work within the police report genre to protect themselves from scrutiny, intending these efforts to result in more social capital, capital that the institution may not always want to grant them. Police departments rarely give officers social capital unless their actions and writing result in cultural and social capital flowing back into the organization. Thus, officers must please the institution in order to be rewarded with more capital.

Officer Lewis noted another constraint on report writing—time. He complained about officers who took too much time or included too much in their reports. During our interview Lewis noted,

> Some people are, you know, extremely detail orientated to where, I believe you need details in there and I get them in there, but at the same time you need to be, you know, pretty efficient with what you do. I mean, you can't be sitting there working on a Domestic Battery for four hours. Do I really

need to know what their past domestic history is? No. You know, when they run their numbers they will see that. And I didn't arrest them for their past domestic battery history. I arrested them for what they were doing that night.

This is a sentiment I heard many times during my research. Officers who hang out in the computer room, rather than on the streets, are often taunted by their peers. There is pressure on officers from all levels (department, supervisor, and other officers) to not spend too much time on reports so that they can get back on the street and assist other officers on calls. The constraint of time is both disciplining and disciplinary. It is used as a means of pressuring officers to return to the street where they are needed by their colleagues. Officers who are seen as spending too much time writing reports are disciplined by other officers, through their taunts or resentment of time-consuming writing practices. However, the restraint on time means that officers may not be spending the time they want to, or need to, on each report. Looking to avoid sanctions and resentment, they may slight report writing by not spending the time they actually need in order to write a good report.

A constraint that Officer Lewis did not mention, but that several other officers expressed, is civil liability. The US Supreme Court case *Bivens v. Six Unknown Named Agents of the Federal Bureau of Narcotics* holds that an officer acting for the department or agency can be sued civilly for violating a person's constitutional rights. This finding means that officers can be sued personally for an action they take while working in their official capacity, potentially losing their homes, savings, and careers in the process. A survey of 600 officers in one southern state found that 27 percent of officers had been personally sued, and 62 percent knew an officer who had been sued (Hall et al., 535). In the same survey, researchers found that 27 percent of police officers believed that the threat of litigation hindered their ability to perform job duties (544). Anecdotally, my husband and I paid out of pocket each year for insurance that would help pay for his defense were he to be sued while working as a police officer. We also knew officers who were sued civilly while working for the Jackson Police Department. The Supreme Court ruling protects citizens from violations of civil rights and allows for restitution if such a violation is made; however, this ruling may also act as a constraint on objective report writing if officers consciously or subconsciously are afraid of being personally and civilly liable for circumstances they may reveal in reports.

THE NARRATIVE

The following is the official police report narrative that was approved for inclusion in Officer Lewis's final report. How the report narrative is written and why Officer Lewis makes specific choices in his writing are the critical concerns of this chapter.[3]

On July 21, 2011 at approximately 2252 hours I responded to the residence at 4-- ------ Avenue reference a disturbance. Upon my arrival I was met at the door by a[n] individual who was not involved in the disturbance advising me that both suspects were located in the bedroom. Both suspects were not involved in a physical fight at the time of my arrival and were separated to conduct interviews.

I first spoke with the female suspect, Pamela F-----, who provided a written statement regarding the incident. Pamela stated that the relationship between her and her boyfriend, Michael G-----, is an abusive one. She stated that Michael was accusing her of cheating and called her a "disgusting whore." Pamela said she tried to not argue with Michael but he continued the verbal abuse. She stated that Michael grabbed her and at that point she sprayed him with "wasp spray" out of self-defense. Pamela stated Michael then began throwing things around the room, attacked her a few more times, and hit her in the head. It should be noted that Pamela had a bruise on her lower back and a bump on her head. Pamela stated she was unsure when during the altercation she obtained the injuries. Photographs were taken of her injuries.

I then spoke with the male suspect, Michael G-----, who stated that they were in an argument and that she was accusing him of cheating. Michael stated they were lying in bed and she sprayed him with "wasp spray." He stated she sprayed him in the face and he got up and started throwing stuff around because he could not see. He stated as he was attempting to leave she continued to spray him. Michael was not aware of how Pamela obtained her injuries but stated he did not hit her. It should be noted that Michael had had red, water eyes form [sic] the wasp spray. There was a large amount of wasp spray on the bed as well as the walls. Photographs of the location of the wasp spray were taken.

Due to the fact that I was unable to determine who was the primary aggressor [sic] was and both parties sustained minor injuries from the altercation both parties were taken into custody. Michael G----- and Pamela F----- were jailed at J----- County Sheriff's Office for Domestic Battery 3rd Degree (5-26-305). The wasp spray used in the incident was logged into evidence. No further information to report at this time. (Lewis, police report)

As Lewis began writing the narrative of the report, I noticed that he was using the first-person pronoun, "I." I asked him why he used "I" in the report and explained that I had seen other officers use "officer," "reporting officer," or even "RO" instead. He stated, "I always write it first person. I mean, I was the one with the story here. It is, you know, my recollection of what happened. I'm the one that went there. I'm the one that made the arrest. I'm going to be the one, you know, testifying later on in court." I asked him what he thought the audience would think about the use of "I" in police reports. He explained,

I mean if you are sitting there reading it, it kinda lays you out a picture like maybe you are putting yourself in their shoes. Basically, what you want to do is paint as pretty a picture as you can for the judge, and the lawyers, and you know, the people involved and, basically, the best account of what they said happened and why you made your arrest.

Lewis, in the narrative section of the report, seizes an opportunity to claim authority and place himself in the "agent function" (Herndl and Licona). He clearly understands his motive for using first person in his reports and wants his audience to know that he takes ownership of the report and his efforts on scene. He is attempting to interact with readers and invite them into "his shoes" in the report, but perhaps it would be more effective for him to think about putting the audience into the shoes of the suspects/victims.

INTERTEXTUALITY AND THE POLICE REPORT

After the first paragraph, which included time, date, and address, Officer Lewis stopped and reread the suspects' written statements. As he began typing, I noticed that he was using the woman's written statement almost verbatim in his own narrative of the events. By contrast, some officers prefer to use the information they obtain from direct question and response during interviews on scene. I asked him why he was relying so heavily on her written statement instead of his own conversation with her on scene. He responded,

> It is nice when there is a written statement cause you're not trying to recollect what everybody said, and well you know, did he say that? You have a firsthand account of what they said happened. If I can do it, and like on hers it is a pretty good written statement, what I do is, I will write my report and my account of what she told me based off of her written statement.

There are very few, if any, quotations in the report that document the interaction Lewis had with the woman outside of her written statement. He justifies the lack of one-on-one conversation with the individuals in the report by claiming that the written statements back up what he says in the report, a closed loop of written and spoken testimony. The intertextuality surprised me in this instance because the report is written as if Lewis had questioned the suspect and she had answered him. However, in reality, she wrote down her version of what happened that night, and Lewis simply used her statement as his own recollection of a conversation that did not actually occur as presented. He was, in effect, plagiarizing her statement as his own narrative. I found this surprising, and worried about the way in which this practice allowed the suspect/victim to speak only through the "voice" of the officer. The implications of such action are even more dramatic due to the fact that the officer is male and the writer is female.

About written statements Lewis explained, "I like it because it is in writing. It provides a recollection of what actually happened later on when they go to court. So whenever somebody is sitting there saying, well, why isn't your story matching up with this later on down the line, it can kinda help the judges." Lewis gives value to the written statement of the suspects over his own recollection of verbal conversations with the two parties. He does this because he thinks there is more value in the written document than in his recollection of their conversations. This is presented against the backdrop of "somebody," who I assume is a prosecutor or defense lawyer, and "judges." Lewis may be anticipating that lawyers and judges prefer written statements over an officer's recollection of conversation. He is making judgments about his audience and adapting the police report in accordance with his beliefs about what the audience values. However, these are assumptions and may not be based on what judges and attorneys actually prefer.

I noticed that in addition to using "I" for himself, Lewis referred to the two suspects in the report by their first names. I asked him why. He remarked,

> I don't know, first names are more personal. Uh, I think maybe if it goes to trial by jury, uh, you know. A lot of people do use last name and date of birth [using robotic voice] and la la la. But I don't really like to do that. When I write my reports, I like them to look like I'm writing a story.

By using first names and first-person perspective, Lewis rejects a facet of the police report genre that he deems robotic. He humanizes the people in the report and tries to interact with the audience. Paint a picture. Tell the story. He is cognizant of a future jury that may read this report and discredit him as an uncaring or, even, a dehumanized officer. In this part of the interview, he recalls that other officers do practice that style of report writing, and he wants to consciously reject and move away from that style. He does not question whether a jury or lawyer may find him too personal or casual in his reports. He assumes that the audience prefers casual, personal narratives to precise, detached ones. This, of course, contradicts his use of the suspects' statements and his style of report writing, which he admits is his "standard outline." His understanding of audience, and what they may or may not want, contradicts his actual writing practice.

Lewis again states that this report may end up in court, something I heard from him several times in our interview. However, while this is obviously something he is concerned about, very few officers appear frequently in court to testify. In fact, Kevin Chapman, a Jackson PD officer with over fifteen years of experience, told me that "an overwhelming majority of cops don't testify in court on a regular basis." The fear of testifying, however, remains an ingrained power that constrains and shapes police reports. Kahneman suggests it is possible to learn fear "by words rather than by experience" (238). I think this is accomplished quite often through police lore, stories, and training. Fear of being cross-examined, even when an officer has never actually experienced cross-examination, can impact how an officer writes a police report. The fear of appearing foolish or incompetent in court is based on the real risk of losing social capital within the institution should such an event occur.

As Lewis began to conclude the woman's side of the story, I asked him if he would include in the report how upset she was about being arrested. He responded,

> No . . . If they are in the back seat of the car spouting off something like "next time I'll hit her harder" or something like that, then yeah. But, you know, she was arrested for domestic battery. She was upset. Why she was upset? She might have been upset she was going to jail, might have been upset 'cause she messed up, might have been upset 'cause she really was the victim in this incidence, but it is impossible for me to

determine who the victim was. And you know State of Arkansas states, if it is visible [injury] we have to make an arrest. It would be unfair of me to take Michael to jail and not her. He has a face full of Raid [wasp spray].

Officer Lewis feels bound in this situation to arrest both parties because he believes the State of Arkansas demands that he do so. He gives several reasons why the woman may have been upset, but including the fact of her demeanor in the report is dismissed as unnecessary. He makes no assumption that he will remember this fact later on, or that it might be brought up by a defense attorney, despite her claim that she will be discussing the unfair arrest with her lawyer. Lewis feels compelled by the State to make the arrest, and he defends his position through the use of the police report genre. The system limits his choices in this arrest, or at least that is how he justifies his decision.

Lewis concluded the woman's paragraph by stating that photographs were taken of her injuries. I asked him if it was important to put in the report that photographs were taken. He responded,

Yeah, because that way, you know, someone is reading it later on, you know, they want to see how serious the injuries are, they see that we have them [photographs] on file. And you know, I add the intake sheet and the photo log, and all this goes in the report. And then I guess they make paper copies of all these in records. I'm not real sure what they do.

Perhaps during training, Lewis has learned to put the statement that "photographs were taken" into his reports, but he has little clarity about how the photos will get pulled and used by lawyers or others down the line. If he knew how difficult it was for the prosecutor to pull the photographs from evidence, he might include much more detail about the injuries in his report. Because Lewis assumes that the evidence is easy to pull, and that all of the readers have easy access to the evidence mentioned in the report, he includes little detail for the readers. This will prove problematic later in the literacy event chain.

Lewis moved on to his next paragraph, which covered the man's perspective of what happened in the incident. I asked him if he was thinking about the prosecutor as he was writing, and how he will be able to determine the primary aggressor. Lewis explained,

> Yeah . . . you want be as extremely detailed as possible. Well, I'm not even as detailed. I'm trying to make it something that I can read before I go into court. And I'm not going to get up there and get hammered by a defense attorney or something. [In lawyer-like voice] "Well, you said it was bug spray here and now it is wasp spray. Which one was it?" I want the facts to be in there, but I want it to be extremely uncomplicated.

Even though my initial question was about the prosecutor, Lewis moves immediately to himself and a defense attorney as the readers of the report. He is most concerned about being embarrassed on the stand and being ridiculed by a defense attorney. Lewis is not thinking so much about the needs of the audience at this point in the report as he is about trying not to embarrass himself. This is especially ironic because Lewis admits in his interview that he has yet to go to court and face cross-examination. His ideas about defense attorney questioning are based on fear, hearsay, and police lore. Consumed by fears of unlikely future court appearances, Officer Lewis focuses on how the report will serve him rather than how it will serve victims or other readers. He is being "rewarded and sanctioned," to use the quote that started this chapter, to focus on what happens in a potential court case. He will be rewarded (with social capital) if he can defend himself well in his written report. However, he will be sanctioned by the system if the report enables a defense attorney to "hammer" him on the stand.

As Lewis wrapped up the report, I asked him about his supervisor as a reader of the report. He claimed that supervisors understand that officers write differently, and that he didn't really consider his supervisor as he was writing. He suggested, "He [supervisor] is just looking for the same thing that you need in a report. The same information." Lewis assumes that the supervisor, as a member of the audience, is on his team and wants the report to include whatever Lewis deems important enough to include. There is little fear or uncertainty about the supervisor reading the report. This is interesting, though, because earlier Lewis claimed that reports are kicked back (by supervisors) even when the officers think they are sufficient, a form of sanction from the system. Perhaps because his supervisor is a fellow officer, Officer Lewis thinks he understands the needs of that particular reader.

I asked Lewis about the witnesses who were on the scene and if he would include any information about them in the report. He argued, "Since they are not willing to do a written statement and tell me what happened, I am just basically going to leave them out. . . . I want my report to show basically what these two people [the arrested suspects] said happened." Lewis included no information at all about the witnesses in the report. There are no names or contact information for them. He also left out that one of the witnesses heard the woman scream, "Don't hit me. Don't hit me." By leaving out this information, he dismisses any interest that the prosecutor or defense may have in being able to call these two people later on and ask for their testimony. In addition, by leaving out witness interviews and declarations (with or without an official written statement), Lewis deprives future readers in the literacy event chain of information they may need to make a decision. There is not a clear sense that he is including all the information and letting the reader come to his or her own conclusion. Lewis says very little about what he saw, heard, asked, or responded to on the scene. This can make a murky situation, like this one where both parties are arrested, even more difficult for the court to resolve.

Finally, I asked Lewis if he was including anything specifically for the prosecutor. He replied,

No. No . . . I mean everyone involved from the prosecutor to the officer to everybody involved, we are going to want the same information. You know, what happened, and what did you do to resolve it basically. And then also when it does go to trial, are you going to be able to recollect what happened? Are the prosecutor and judge going to be able to read your report and have a pretty good picture of what happened? And you know to cover yourself. This woman was saying that I made an unlawful arrest and that she would be talking to her attorney about this. So, you know, also a lot of what you do is CYA [cover your ass]. You want a good reason and a good recollection of why both parties were arrested on a domestic battery.

Officer Lewis claims that he is writing for the purpose of mnemonic or memorial writing. He does this thinking of an imaginary time when he might have to go to court, even though this rarely happens. It is solipsistic. Police officers know the audience and can name specific readers, but they don't know what those readers expect or want; or if they do, they ignore this in order to write for their own purposes and to, as Lewis explains, CYA.

A COMPLEX AND CONTESTED GENRE

Officer Lewis needs this police report to serve multiple audiences and purposes. This reality is at the heart of the police report genre and is what makes it such a complex genre with seemingly competing interests. Miller argues that "what we learn when we learn a genre is not just a pattern of forms or even a method of achieving our own ends. We learn, more importantly, what ends we may have" (165). I would add that genre in many cases also teaches us what ends *we may not have*, and this knowledge is incredibly valuable when it comes to critiquing and analyzing the police report genre. Officer Lewis is not allowed in the genre to admit his own fault, to expose a mistake, or to include information that does not support his ultimate decision to arrest. It would be against his own self-interest to do so, and thus, against the generic requirements of a police report. I have yet to read a report in which the officer admits to forgetting to read a suspect Miranda rights or notes failing to ask consent before entering a home. Police reports are used as much to bolster and justify the actions of an officer as they are to describe the who, what, when, where, and how of an event. The report supports the ideal image of Officer Lewis as a "good" and "objective" police officer, thereby providing him with the social capital he needs to be successful as a police officer and proving his competency.

Much of what Lewis is doing in the report is explaining, justifying, and defending the reasons for his own actions. Because both parties are arrested, he needs to justify his decision in the report by stating that each person has injuries. The inclusion of the witness report that the woman screamed, "Don't hit me. Don't hit me" would not help him in reasoning that each party was aggressive and attacked the other. In the interview, along with admitting the report is a means to "CYA," Officer Lewis also describes the report as a mnemonic device. He mentions at several points in the interview the importance of remembering the event details. Whenever he mentions the report's work as a memorial tool, this is quickly followed by a statement about a possible future court date. Previous sanctions or warnings from supervisors about how defense attorneys use reports is disciplining his report writing and shaping this narrative. It could also be that simply hearing the horror stories of other officers who have been "hammered" on the stand or sued civilly has convinced Officer Lewis to write a report that is more about self-preservation, remembering detail, and choosing simplicity over complexity, and less about being helpful to readers in the literacy event chain.

Lewis wants a report that will ultimately provide him with social and cultural capital. It is a professional document written in a professional manner with detail paid to specific vocabulary and style. While Lewis claims he is avoiding robotic-sounding police jargon in his report, the use of modals and nominals in phrases such as "reference a disturbance," and "it should be noted," distance him from the action in the report. Despite his use of the first person, he is also oddly missing from sentences such as "Photographs were taken of her injuries"; "The wasp spray used in the incident was logged into evidence"; and "No further information to report at this time." Lewis's use of passive voice and other techniques places him firmly within the expectations of the police report genre, even though he rejects using a robotic voice. He has been rewarded, then, by the department and the hierarchal literacy event chain for writing reports in this style, even though he openly states that he wants to humanize his interactions with citizens.

The constraints of a police report, in this example, and the police report genre, in general terms, may keep Officer Lewis from writing a truly reflective and objective document. The police report genre allows him to highlight information that supports his decision to arrest while leaving out information that contradicts that decision. The disciplining nature of the genre, previous sanctions from supervisors, and warnings in the form of stories told by other officers lead Lewis to write a document that he believes will strengthen his identity as a police officer and will gain him social capital. If his agency in this act of report writing can result in greater competency in writing the kinds of reports that protect him from scrutiny and raise his social capital, he will likewise gain cultural capital. In the following chapters, Lewis's police report will be examined by other readers, readers who need to use the report for their own purposes and gain their own capital.

Micro-Chapter

Bad Day

OFFICER JOHN SEAWRIGHT ARRIVED AT 1226 W. Main in Jackson at 8:00 in the morning.

"Hey, thanks for coming out so quickly," a young man said as he walked up to John in the driveway. "I'm Steve Reed. I'm the one that called the police department." He extended his hand, and John shook it as he looked toward the house. The screen door of the home was open, and John could see glass on the porch from the broken window in the front door.

"So tell me what happened," John said as he took a pad of paper from the pocket of his uniform. The man replied, "I work the night shift over at the plant. I left the house about 9:30 last night and I came back this morning at 7:30 and found it like this."

John shook his head. He hated working burglaries. The invasion of a home is very upsetting to residents, and it is one of those crimes that is very rarely solved. With most burglaries, there is not enough evidence or information to find the person or persons responsible.

"Okay. Why don't you show me around, and I can look for fingerprints," John told the man. They both went through the door and began looking room to room for evidence. The two-way radio affixed to John's shoulder clicked on, and he heard his officer number called out by the dispatcher. He walked a few feet away from the owner of the home and responded to the dispatcher.

She said, "Hey, that guy, Steve Reed? Is he with you now?" John replied that he was. The dispatcher continued, "Well, he has a warrant for his arrest in Jackson."

John took a deep breath and blew it out slowly. He responded, "Okay. I will take him to county. Let them know we're coming."

John turned back to Steve and said, "Man, I hate to do this, but they just told me you have a warrant for your arrest. I gotta take you to the county jail."

Steve replied, "Yeah, I knew I had one. Yeah. Okay. Let's do that now, so I can bond out and work tonight."

John reemphasized, "Man, I am sorry. You call us out for a burglary and I have to take you in. That is a bad day, man. I am so sorry."

Back at the department, John wrote up the report for the burglary and included Steve Reed's warrant arrest in the narrative. In the report he tried to be as sympathetic toward Steve as possible because although Steve was the victim of a burglary, he had ended up in jail that day. A couple of hours later, John's supervisor found him in the police department.

"Hey, I need you to change that warrant arrest report," the supervisor told John, stopping him in the hallway.

John replied, "Okay, what is it?"

"You say in the report 'Unfortunately, Steve Reed had a warrant and I had to place him under arrest.' What is that? You can't do that. No one cares what you felt at the time. The guy had a warrant. You placed him under arrest. Period," his supervisor reprimanded him.

John tried to explain. "No, I went to the guy's house for a burglary and he was the victim. I had to arrest him when dispatch told me he had a warrant. Guy had a terrible day—his house is broken into, and then he goes to jail. Man, I just felt bad for the guy."

John's supervisor looked up from the report with steely eyes. "John, you can't have emotion in your reports. It is just the facts. That is all. Change it."

John took the report from his supervisor's outstretched hand. "Okay. You got it," he replied.

∽

A particularly thorny issue in police reports is the objective stance required of officers. The report genre and officer training demands that officers be objective, factual, clear, and concise in their report writing. They are continually reminded to remove language or details that create a subjective impression. In the previous account, the officer wanted to express his empathy for a man he saw as a victim of one crime, yet the perpetrator of another. His own conflicted feelings about the warrant arrest made him bend the parameters of the police report genre so that he could include his disappointment in having to arrest the man.

It may be difficult for officers to dismiss their affect when writing reports. This is especially true for violent crimes, crimes against children, and other complicated circumstances they encounter. Brand notes that it is basically impossible to remove or pretend to remove all emotion from one's writing (438). Yet officers are asked to do this every day, despite the highly emotional jobs they perform. As we saw in the previous chapter with Officer Lewis, the objective stance that is taught and required in the police report genre is in direct conflict with how officers see their writing process.

Officer Lewis described writing a report as "painting a picture." I hear this description of report writing along with "telling the story" constantly in academy report-writing classes. These phrases imply creativity, storytelling, narrative, the selection of some details and the omission of others. Painting a picture also assumes a mood, an emotion, and an artist. It is understandable that officers may feel confused when they are encouraged to "paint the picture" and then asked to remove all of the affect from reports. The genre requirements are often in direct conflict with what officers think they are supposed to be doing in their reports.

Brandt's investigation into the writing that occurs in workplaces across the country exposes the complex contexts of those who write for pay. She argues, "Most strikingly, they [people who write documents for employers] write in contexts where normative notions of authorship in U.S. society, including a long tradition of respecting the personality and expressive rights of individual writers, do not pertain" (*The Rise of Writing* 24). The requirements of objective facts and emotionless expression of detail are incredibly difficult for officers to meet. As people who write for pay, officers are instructed to create a-rhetorical, objective reports, a standard that cannot exist in reality.

2

The Creation and Circulation of Cultural and Social Capital

> We need reminding that the very idea of being both human and
> impartial is a contradiction in terms.
>
> —Brand 438–39

OFFICERS AT THE JACKSON POLICE DEPARTMENT ARE required to have all of their police reports completed within the same work shift.[1] The reports are then read and critiqued by a supervising officer, typically the sergeant or lieutenant on duty. The supervising officers work at the police station, rather than on the street, and review reports as they come in through the Jackson PD police report database. Supervisors return the reports to officers during the same shift for corrections and revisions. Supervisors are the first readers of reports beyond the officer, the first link in the literacy event chain. They have the final say in whether a report is ready to be officially submitted and read by others.

Tom Cuddy was the supervising officer on duty the night of Officer Lewis's domestic disturbance call (see Chapter 1). Sergeant Cuddy has been an officer with the Jackson PD for sixteen years and was promoted to sergeant four years ago. His responsibilities include conducting the daily pre-shift meeting; assigning officers to their city zone each shift; backing up officers; making critical decisions on important calls during the shift; and approving every officer's reports. He is kind, friendly, and soft-spoken. He is well liked by his officers and has a pleasant demeanor.

Officer Lewis turned in his report at 2:00 a.m. I entered Sergeant Cuddy's office a few minutes later and asked if he could go over the report with me. His office was constructed of cubicle panels covered in light blue tweed fabric. There were four such cubicles in the room. A picture of Cuddy's son in a baseball uniform sat next to his computer. The partition wall behind the computer was only a half wall, so the office had no privacy, but most officers were out on patrol at the time of our interview, and the station was eerily quiet.

Sergeant Cuddy greeted me warmly, shook my hand, and asked me to sit in a chair he had pulled in from one of the other cubicle offices. He looked at the large flat-screen monitor in front of him and logged onto the Jackson PD database. Scrolling through the "reports awaiting approval" screen, he found Officer Lewis's report.

COP TALK

I asked Cuddy what he looked for when reading officers' reports. He explained, "I am just looking for the basics. You know, who, what, when, where, why, and how. Okay? And on top of that, I look for the elements of the crime to make sure they have those in there." This suggests that Cuddy understands a prosecutor will be reading the report, and that he needs to identify the elements of the crime and compare those to the legal statute. When I asked Officer Lewis about the prosecutor, he seemed to think the prosecutor needed the same information the supervisor and officer needed. Even when I specifically asked Lewis about whether he would include the elements of the crime from the statutes, he responded, "Well, you know, I don't have all the statutes in my head." Officer Lewis did not seem to share his sergeant's concern for including the legal definition and elements of the charges.

Sergeant Cuddy continued,

> It needs to be understood by anybody. Okay? And, you know, we tell them no cop talk. You know, no acronyms. All those need to be spelled out. . . . It [the report] should be able to be understood by anyone that picks it up. Should be able to sit here and read it. They should be able to follow it in sequence from the time the officer was dispatched from dispatch to the time that whatever the resolution of the case was, arrest or whatever it was.

The first thing Cuddy complains about is "cop talk." I assume that this is the same kind of language and style that Officer Lewis disregards and tries to avoid in his own report. This also suggests, though, that Cuddy believes the report audience will include regular citizens, because lawyers and judges would be familiar with legal and police officer jargon. While jury members and other citizens may need to be able to read the report and understand it, for a misdemeanor arrest, it is very unlikely that the case will ever go to trial, especially a trial by jury. Most misdemeanor cases are decided by a judge, usually after the prosecutor and defense attorney agree on a plea deal. Rarely do misdemeanor cases go to trial and require the officer and witnesses to testify. That a jury member will be reading this report in the future is highly unlikely, especially because reports aren't technically reviewed by a jury or judge. In the case of a trial, the officer's testimony about the event (often recalled based on the report he or she reads while testifying) is what the judge and jury would consider, not the actual report itself.

I redirected Cuddy's response back to the original question about the prosecutor. I asked him specifically if he was looking for anything in the report that a prosecutor would need to know. He responded,

> Well, yes and no. And the reason I say that is for us to make an arrest we need probable cause. For the prosecutors, they are looking at beyond a reasonable doubt. When I'm looking at it, I have to make sure that, like if an arrest was made, there was probable cause to make the arrest. For the guys to make an arrest there has to be certain standards. As far as misdemeanors, you can't make a misdemeanor arrest without a warrant unless it falls into five categories: a domestic battery, a misdemeanor that happened in your presence, shoplifting where the person was detained by loss prevention, so there are certain standards. [He listed only three of the five exceptions in the interview.] I have to make sure that all that stuff is in here. I'm looking at it for as far as when they go to court, if it is a good report for them [the officer]. They need it to refresh their memory, and I have to be able to understand it whether

I was out there or not. By reading their report I should know exactly what happened.

Cuddy mentions the importance of the officer as a reader of his or her own report. He considers it part of his job as a supervisor to ensure that the officer, as an audience member of his or her own report, has a "good report." He emphasizes that the report should refresh the memory of the officer and not necessarily include information that is critical for the prosecutor. Cuddy seems more concerned about protecting the officer's recollection of the incident and his or her probable cause for the arrest in the report than including information a prosecutor or judge may need. This is in line with Officer Lewis's view of the report as an important mnemonic tool. In addition, Cuddy seems to share Officer Lewis's preoccupation with going to court. It is a topic he brings up several times in our short interview, stressing the need for officers to have reports that in essence protect them from cross-examination, or at the very least, provide them with the details they need to remember from the event. Cuddy tries to ensure that the officers have cultural capital (knowledge, competency) and social capital (reputation, status) when they appear in court. Having a good report will help officers retain these forms of capital.

"UNIFORM" STANDARD ENGLISH

As Cuddy prepared to read the narrative of the report, I asked him about the most frequent reasons for rejecting a report. He replied that he usually kicked back reports for "minor grammar and errors." This concern stems from the belief that poor grammar in a report reflects badly on the officer and the department.

Cuddy explained that he needed to read the report narrative several times because,

> Depending on how somebody [pause] what kind of school they went to, the extent of their education, they write different. And we have some Hispanic officers where their primary language is Spanish, so then you have to go through it. Sometimes, you know, they get their adjectives in the wrong place

or something like that, and it doesn't flow, you know. Not just them, you know, people when they are typing they get in a hurry, and they are thinking what they want to say but leave out crucial elements. So, I read pretty slow and deliberately.

Cuddy emphasizes that he is focused on grammar and the readability of a report. He wants the report to "flow." Though he wants the critical elements to be there, his main concern seems to be making sure the report will be received as a professional and well-written document. He wants his officers to appear professional in their writing because professionalism is important to the department and the larger organization. It brings the officer (and the organization) social capital.

Cuddy is also concerned about particular kinds of writers—bilingual officers and those with low levels of education. Officers must not only wear the uniform of the department on their bodies, but also wear Uniform Standard English (as determined by the supervisor and department) in their writing. The strict requirement and expectation of Uniform Standard English jeopardizes an officer's own agency and voice in his or her reports, but it may do more than just reduce agency. Cuddy, without saying it, is requesting officers to produce a text that sounds "white," that is devoid of any other markers—a raced discourse. He catches himself discussing what he deems as deficiencies (or at least the crosslinguistic influences) of his Latinx officers, and quickly notes that other people also make mistakes when they write reports.

Beyond the language used in reports, the genre demands an a-historical and objective stance. The request that every report include the who, what, when, where, and how without relating historical information, emotionality, and perspective signals a white, and more specifically, a white-masculine rhetoric. Officer Seawright, the officer in the story that preceded this chapter, is asked to remove his affect from a police report in which he was trying to display his regret in having to arrest a citizen. Cuddy, in this chapter, asks bilingual officers to remove the traces of crosslinguistic influences from their reports. Both Officer Seawright and Officer Lewis are conflicted by these requests because both men want to tell the story of what happened from their perspective. The demands of their supervisors and the genre cause tension between the officers' desire to write subjective reports and the restraints that call for objective ones, a conflict that seems impossible to resolve.

REQUESTS FOR REPORT REVISIONS

Cuddy starred at the computer screen, silently reading Officer Lewis's narrative, and remarked,

> He [officer] needs to be a little more specific about what he [suspect] did that she is saying was self-defense. Because here, he [officer] says she has a bruise on her lower back. So how did she obtain that bruise? Was she thrown down? Did he hit her in the back? Did he kick her in the back? You know, how did she get that bruise? How did she explain that bruise? And the same way with the bump on her head. Those are the main things that I noticed. I didn't see anything else.

Sergeant Cuddy does not note any grammar or style errors, even though this is what he claimed to look for in reports. He recommends that the officer include more details in the report on how the woman obtained her injuries.

When I look at the original rough draft (the version Cuddy saw for this interview) and the final report (the one eventually approved and logged into Records), it is clear to me that Lewis included only one sentence in response to this review. After Lewis describes the woman's injuries in the report, he adds, "Pamela stated she was unsure when during the altercation she obtained the injuries." This does not seem to answer Cuddy's request for more detail on the injury. Because Lewis took no notes at the scene of his interview with the woman and relied only on her written statement in the report, he may not know how she obtained the injuries. Despite the report seemingly depicting a conversation between Lewis and the woman, the report merely restates what she claims happened in her written statement. This could be a serious problem with the report, because the officer may not have asked for specific details or may not recall the woman's response when asked about her injuries.

I asked Cuddy if the two witnesses who were on the scene should have been included in the report. He responded,

> I would put at least their names if they were identified. That is one thing that as I am checking these, he is not the only officer that was there. There were other officers, so there will be supplemental reports coming in. That is one thing that I may ask him. I would ask him, hey did you ID those people, or did someone else? I don't want to seem like I am micromanaging. You know it is something that is important because the prosecutor can ask those people to come in and tell them what happened.

Cuddy understands that details like witness contact information are important to a prosecutor. These witnesses could help identify the primary aggressor in court and help solve a relatively difficult he said/she said case. What Cuddy does not do, however, is ensure that these details are included in the report.

The final report has no mention of witnesses. There are no supplemental reports with this information either. Cuddy mentions that he doesn't want to be seen as "micromanaging." This statement is odd coming from a supervising officer with so many years at the department. Lewis has been an officer for a little over one year. I would think that micromanaging would be common in such cases, and in certain instances, necessary when working with such an inexperienced officer. It is unknown why the requested changes do not appear in the final document. Did the supervisor not review the revised report carefully? Did Sergeant Cuddy tell me what he would want changed but not relay the information to Officer Lewis? Was Cuddy telling me what he thought I might want to hear when asked about specific readers and witness information? Is it simply too difficult for a sergeant on one shift to carefully read reports and the subsequent revisions before approving them?

There were eight officers on duty the night Officer Lewis filed his report. If each officer wrote only one report, Cuddy would have to review eight initial reports and then potentially eight revised reports. He would have to do this within a tight time frame, as every final report must be submitted during the shift. Because we reviewed Lewis's report at 2:00 a.m., the revised report would have been written and approved by 6:00 a.m. in order for it to be submitted to the database in time. Whatever the case, the report in its final form is lacking information the various audience members will need, as is detailed in subsequent interviews with the report readers.

In the case of Lewis's report, agency does not reside in an individual; rather, it "exists at the intersection of a network of semiotic, material, and . . . intentional elements and relational practices" (Herndl and Licona 137). The officer's agency function in writing the report is bolstered, constrained, given away, and abruptly recalled throughout the writing and revision of this report. Blythe points out that "writing is often the nexus in which human agency and institutional constraints get played out" (180). Outside forces, along with internal preferences and beliefs, dictate at which points Lewis exerts his own agency function and at which point he must succumb to other agents. Although Cuddy suggested that the woman's injuries be explained in more detail and that the witnesses' names be included, neither request is adequately addressed or included in the final report. The reason for this is unknown, but it is clear that the report in its final submitted form must have satisfied both the officer and the sergeant.

PROFESSIONALIZATION AND CAPITAL

Officer Lewis and Sergeant Cuddy both argue that reports are critical documents in helping officers remember details, a mnemonic tool that provides a type of cultural capital in the form of competency. This capital not only reflects positively on the officer, but flows back to the department so that the cultural power of a good report makes the entire department appear more credible. Winsor reminds us, "Within a hierarchy, people in more powerful positions are often able to determine what knowledge is valuable and even what facts or ideas are to count as knowledge for the organization" (7). This report accrues value for the officer and the supervisor in that it is deemed by both of them to be a good report for court and a document that provides cultural capital for the department.

In addition to aiding memory, Officer Lewis and Sergeant Cuddy share the belief that reports should be professional and free of police jargon. A professional document equals one that is free of grammatical errors and addresses a civilian audience. The movement to professionalize law enforcement seeks to elevate police work to a more prominent and socially attractive field; with professionalization comes more economic capital (in the form of officer pay) and more social capital (in the form of more prestige for officers and departments). However, professionalization is not an easy task and comes with its own set of problems. The question of *how* to professionalize law enforcement may not be the one to ask. A more interesting question is *why* departments and institutions want to professionalize.

The public criticism of law enforcement creates a type of institutional insecurity for officers and their supervisors. Constant scrutiny from lawyers, judges, media, and the public can create an environment of hyper-awareness and fear of judgment in police departments. This environment may cause both officers and supervisors to focus more on the form of a report than the content. However, this focus on grammar and form actually ends up hurting officers because they aren't focused on other issues in the report. Kevin Chapman, another supervisor at the Jackson PD, told me,

> Sometimes we do things just to try to look professional and it is not really necessary. The officers don't have enough influences and styles of writing or options to choose from. All they know is one and two. [He is referring to the one style of report writing taught in the academy and the other style of report writing presented to new officers by their field training officer.] They are scared to death to change that because they are worried they will get in trouble. Then it just becomes a habit.

Chapman is disappointed that officers don't have more models of the police report genre and are not encouraged to take college courses in English, courses he thinks would broaden officers' writing abilities and understanding of writing. As a composition and technical writing instructor, I would love to agree with him. However, Officer Lewis graduated with a degree in business from a good state university, and he has a good command of writing. His constraints seem to stem more from the expectations of his department and the report genre than from the lack of writing experiences.

Miller notes that in "constructing discourse, we deal with purposes at several levels, not just one. We learn to adopt social motives as ways of satisfying private intentions through rhetorical action" (162). In the case of this report, the officer and supervisor want the report to serve the purpose of a mnemonic tool for a potential court case; a professional report that reflects highly on its writer and his department; and a document that explains to anyone who might read it what occurred on scene. Both the supervisor and Officer Lewis, in the creation and revision of this report, were focused on securing department and officer reputation (social capital) and officer ability (cultural capital). Neither of these men ever mentioned the suspects, the victims, the State of Arkansas, or any outside parties as needing to be served by this document. This is surprising because many, including myself, assume that one of the purposes of a police report is to serve the victim of a crime. In this particular situation, the victim is the State of Arkansas because both parties were arrested. However, due to the nature of this specific event, I think it is more probable that one of those arrested is actually a victim, because it is almost impossible that both the man and the woman started the fight at exactly the same time. This is a point the judge who read this report brings up as well. So while the document should serve the victims in the case, it seems to do very little of that. Report writing, in this example, is an act that demonstrates professionalism, expressed through grammar and answering the who, what, when, where, and how. At this point in the chained literacy event, cultural capital is accrued through the supervisor's review and approval, and this power is circulated back to Officer Lewis in recognition of his competence and knowledge. The officer gains credibility as the report gains approval from Sergeant Cuddy.

In terms of symbolic capital, the report begins to accrue power at the level of supervisor review and approval. Because structure in organizations can exist only if people are constantly engaged in structuring (Giddens), it is imperative that Officer Lewis and Sergeant Cuddy protect their own interests first before considering other readers. Cuddy wants to protect Lewis's reputation and his abilities in a possible trial. Lewis wants to have his report approved in a timely manner, so he writes a report that he hopes will be accepted by his supervisor. Because both already know and understand the constraints of the genre itself—do not admit mistakes, be concise, write observations as facts—the officer and the supervisor recirculate the power in this document back to the institution, namely the Jackson Police Department.

The report gains a kind of agency that moves with it up the chain of command. Devitt reminds us that "genres not only reflect but also reinforce the ideology of the group whose purposes they serve" (*Writing Genres* 60). This is especially true when a genre is created and maintained by institutions that have vast amounts of power, such as police and state systems. As the quotation that began this chapter reminds us, it is impossible to be both human and impartial. Officers want to be sure they are protecting themselves and their departments from criticism and scrutiny. If and how this can be accomplished while writing a report that serves its readers will be addressed in the remaining chapters.

3

Authority, Agency, and the Places of Contested Power

> Genres are a resource that can be deployed, manipulated, contested, and regulated. They are thus a way in which power is constructed, organized and put into effect.
>
> —Winsor 11

EVERY REPORT, ONCE APPROVED BY AN OFFICER'S SUPERVISOR, is sent on to the Records department for distribution to the Jackson city attorney's office or the county district attorney's office. The city attorney prosecutes all traffic and misdemeanor violations. Cases prosecuted by this office would include driving while impaired (DWI), domestic abuse, misdemeanor violent crimes, traffic violations, and misdemeanor fraud. As in many cities, the city attorney in Jackson works very few, if any, actual cases. He or she provides legal advice to the mayor, city council, city offices, and city attorney's office staff. Most of the cases that come to the city attorney's office are actually worked by assistant prosecutors. Mark Guston is one of four assistant prosecutors in Jackson. He has worked as a prosecutor in the office for four years. Prior to his position with the City of Jackson, he worked for three years as a defense attorney at a private firm in Jackson.

Guston, at my request, agreed to review Officer Lewis's report and offer his professional opinion about the report, the incident, and the possible prosecution of the two people named in the report. I met with him approximately one week after the domestic disturbance call. The report had not yet been transferred from the police department to the city attorney's office, or if it had, no assistant prosecutor had yet been assigned to review it.

I arrived at Jackson City Hall, a recently renovated three-story building with a glass façade, and entered the doors meant for public citizens. I carefully made my way to the glass (presumably bullet-proof) window that read "City Attorney." A woman at the desk behind the glass welcomed me and then called Mark Guston to escort me back to his office. Natural light from a wall of windows streamed into his large and comfortable office. He pointed me to one of the leather armchairs in front of his desk. A picture of his boss, the city attorney, was positioned on a shelf behind him. Guston's legal degree and other certificates hung on the wall to my right. It was an environment in stark contrast to that of Sergeant Cuddy, whose office was a half-walled cubicle in a dimly lit room shared with four other people.

I showed Guston the report and told him that I had obtained it as part of a ride-along with the Jackson Police Department.[1] I asked him to use his experience and expertise as a prosecutor to identify any information in the report that was unclear, missing, or extraneous. Guston reviewed all of the attached tickets, written suspect statements, and supporting documents prior to reading the report narrative. He took several minutes looking through the documents, before moving to Lewis's narrative.

He read the report aloud and stopped at points to remark on what he was reading. "Well, the first thing that I read [in the narrative] is that 'I was met at the door by someone not involved in the disturbance.' It would be nice to know who that person is because they could potentially be a witness." The witness concern is something that will be discussed by all subsequent interviewees. The fact that a person is mentioned in the report but not described, named, or identified as a witness is a problem for the judicial audience members of the police report for various reasons. Guston continued to read the narrative aloud, and then remarked,

> It says "Michael grabbed her." Where? Did it leave a mark? Did he grab her once? One hand? Both hands? Were they in the house? Umm. [Reading aloud] "At that point she sprayed him with wasp spray." Did she spray him in the face? In the eye? Did she spray in his direction? Was she ten feet from

him? Was she two feet from him? Umm. [Reading aloud] "Pamela stated Michael then started throwing things around the room." What things? Were there broken things lying around to corroborate her story? [Reading aloud] "Attacked her a few more times." In what way? Verbally? Physically? Umm. [Reading aloud] "And hit her in the head." With what? His hand? With his fist? Open hand? Closed hand? With an item that he was throwing?

Guston wants details about every statement made regarding the battery. How was she grabbed? What things were thrown? Where and how was he sprayed with wasp spray? What was she hit with? The supervisor had asked Lewis to add how the woman was injured, but had not asked for the level of detail requested by the prosecutor. Listening to Guston's responses, I wondered what Officer Lewis would think if he knew how unclear his paragraph was for a prosecutor. I was startled by how differently the prosecutor and the officer viewed the information. It reminded me of how I felt reading the professor's comments on my first graduate paper. I only *thought* I understood the academic research genre and what the instructor expected. Reading the comments, I realized how far I had to go to achieve the actual expectations. If the prosecutor reviewed and gave feedback on police reports such as Officer Lewis's, could it influence officers to improve their reports for that audience much in the same way that teacher feedback on writing assignments improves students' future writing?

ESTABLISHING AUTHORITY

Guston put the report down on his desk and pushed his chair away, as if trying to distance himself from the report itself. I told Guston that there were two witnesses on scene, not just the one that Lewis had mentioned in the report. I had asked Officer Lewis if he was going to name the witnesses in the report, but he had responded that if the prosecutor wanted that, then he would go find them, or maybe she (the victim) would convince one of the witnesses to testify for her.

As soon as I explained Officer Lewis's reasoning, Guston looked up at the ceiling, his face tight with frustration. He looked back at me and said, "Well, see the problem with that is that I'm not an investigator. I'm a prosecutor. So if he is on the scene, and they are standing there, and they are witnesses to a crime, it doesn't really matter if they don't want to talk. They have to give me their name and basic information." I told Guston that I did not believe Lewis took down any contact information from the witnesses. He replied, "And so how am I supposed to find them? Call the two defendants that are represented by council and say 'Hey, who was at the house and saw all this?' . . . Not getting the names of the people that were there and witnessed it is unforgivable. That is just ridiculous."

The officer has clearly not anticipated the needs of the prosecutor as a reader. Guston implies in his interview that by not providing more information, the officer is either incompetent or lazy. He completely dismisses the officer's justification for not identifying the witnesses—the officer felt that because they were uncooperative, they wouldn't provide good information. In addition, the supervisor bears some responsibility for the lack of witness information. Even though the supervisor said he would ask for the inclusion of witness information, it was never included in this or other subsequent supplemental reports. Winsor reports a similar situation when technicians and engineers report on "facts" that are later questioned by their managers. She notes, "When 'facts' were transferred across fields, their relevance and stability became less self-evident. Managers needed to be persuaded that engineers knew what they were talking about" (61). Likewise, while the officer and supervisor agree on what constitutes the facts of the report, the prosecutor remains unsure, and the report details seem unclear. He is not persuaded by the facts in the officer's report and even questions the officer's abilities. The officer is seen as having very little cultural capital in this scenario, despite the fact that he has primary knowledge of the events on scene. The prosecutor doubts the officer's competency and ability to convey the details he requires.

I told Guston, "Now I know that she told the officer that night that she was advised by her attorney to keep wasp spray by her bed for self-defense, which I thought was interesting, but it wasn't included in the report. The witnesses also heard her say, 'Don't hit me. Don't hit me.' But that is not in the report."

Guston shifted his weight in his chair, leaned over his desk toward me, and remarked, "The witnesses heard her say as it was going on, 'Don't hit me. Don't hit me'?" He continued,

> I can't imagine how that is not relevant. I mean, again, it takes it from a he said/she said to witnesses. When you have a case like this, anything beyond what the two parties say is hugely important. We absolutely need to know who these witnesses are. I don't care if they don't want to talk. The problem is this: you really can't give me too much information. There is really no such thing when you are prosecuting a case. Because if the defense attorney gets some information and shows up with a witness who says they saw it all, and I say, "Well I didn't know there was a witness," they are going to say, "Well they were there. Cop didn't want to ask them any questions." That makes me look like a dumbass. Which makes him [the officer] look like a dumbass. Which makes me angry. Which makes me call supervising officers and have conversations about that officer's level of training. Maybe they need to go back and have a little refresher course. I can't really think of anything more egregious than having a witness to something and not even getting their contact information. I mean, if they didn't want to talk at the time, you at least get their contact information so that I can put them under prosecutor subpoena and get them in here and question them myself.

It is fascinating that Guston highlights how this report has the power to make him (and the officer) "look like a dumbass." The thought of being embarrassed by a defense or other attorney worries him as he reviews this report and realizes how the missing information could reflect badly on him. As the report moves along the chain of command, the ethos of the writer is transferred to the supervisor and the prosecutor. The transfer of ethos, however, is unwelcome when it lacks cultural and social capital or substantive authority. A powerful report in terms of cultural and social capital will increase the capital of the supervisor and prosecutor, while a poor report will have the opposite effect.

Guston is quick to note that if he looks like a "dumbass," the officer will follow quickly behind. The fact that Guston will ask the supervisor "about that officer's level of training" represents a threat to the officer's own reputation and position (social capital). Guston makes it clear that if a report makes him look bad, he will make the officer who wrote it suffer with him. Of course, the supervisor will also be held accountable, because the officer is under his management. The chained literacy event links all of these men together, each relying on the other for his own claim of legitimacy and authority. The report can circulate cultural and social capital up the chain to bolster the prosecutor, or it can result in diminished capital and embarrass him. The report then has symbolic power to prop up or pull down the chained readers depending on its ethos, cultural capital, and social capital.

Guston acknowledges that he can't get too much information in a police report. This statement begs another point, which is that perhaps he *can't ever get enough* information. This creates a very difficult space for officers to operate in. It is impossible to create an a-rhetorical document or a truly objective report, yet the prosecutor seems to demand this while at the same time insisting on extensive detail that will answer any potential question that he might need to ask. The constraints of time, individual perception, rhetorical stance, fear, and inherent paradox of the report genre prevent officers from ever being able to deliver such a report. Police officers' own interactions with prosecutors, defense attorneys, and supervisors also shape their observations and reporting. The fear of court, of damaging their reputation, or of admitting a mistake can affect what is included and not included in the final report narrative. In turn, an officer's decision making and credibility are open to being criticized by those in positions higher than his or her own, and cultural and social capital is lost.

Clearly, Officer Lewis and Sergeant Cuddy have drastically underestimated the amount of information and detail requested by the prosecutor, but why?

Guston offered one explanation in his interview.

There is some substance here of, well, it is just a misdemeanor. Nobody really got hurt. Well, okay. I get that. But if that is the attitude, then don't arrest them. Don't charge them. Don't add a case to my caseload that I've got a he said/she said, and I could have had witnesses that could have made it easy to plea or easy to try. Now I've got a shitty case on the docket, and all it looks like is the prosecutor is dismissing domestic batteries. I mean, if you don't care enough to put the time into doing that, and I'm not saying that you should or shouldn't. Some of these are just a bunch of bullshit and the best thing to do is tell one of them to leave the house and work it out. But if you are going to write a report and you are going to arrest them, spend an extra ten minutes putting the right information in the report.

Guston is concerned about his caseload being filled with cases he has to dismiss because they are not cases that he will be able to successfully prosecute. This scenario can make a prosecutor appear weak to the public. A poor report creates an investigative problem for the prosecutor's office and a public relations headache.

The authority of the prosecutor, a position higher than the officer in the chain of hierarchy, is in conflict with the authority granted by the system to the officer to create a report based on the officer's observations. Guston questions the ethos of the report, especially the rhetorical choices the officer makes in including and not including specific evidence. This inherent conflict is complicated further by the fact that the prosecutor is not really in a position to ask the officer for revision, unlike the supervisor. So while the prosecutor is in a position of authority, given his appointment as a prosecutor by the mayor, he actually has very little ability to influence how reports are written. One possible solution would be for Guston to visit the department and speak with supervisors about police report training, but even then, officers and supervisors could ignore his requests and continue writing reports in whatever way they like. This reality may explain why the prosecutor is so upset by this report—it has the symbolic power to reduce his social capital, but there is very little he can do to influence report-writing practices, despite his position of authority.

THE RULES OF DISCOVERY

I informed Guston that the woman involved in this incident was upset and had threatened to call her attorney and file charges against the officer. I asked Guston if he would want that information in the report. He replied,

> I mean look, the rules of discovery are pretty simple. Rule 17.1, 17.2, 17.3, if a defendant makes a statement and it's not contained in discovery, I don't get to talk about it. If I send this police report and these [Pamela's and Michael's] written statements to the defense attorney, and they look at it and say, "Fine. We are going to trial on it," and I show up and the cop gets on the stand and starts saying, "Well, she also told me . . ." Buzzzzz. Red buzzer goes off. He doesn't get to say that. I don't care if it is in his field notes. I don't care where it is written, or if he remembers it that day. I have to give any defendant or their attorney the substance of any statements made by that person [the officer]. If I don't give them to them, I don't get to use them. Now they can get their witness, their client, their defendant on the stand, and they can say whatever they want. If the defendant gets up there and tells a whole different version of the story, then guess what? Then the defense attorney—which is exactly what I would do if I were the defense attorney—recalls the cop, because I, as the prosecutor, don't get to bring that information out. But the defense attorney can put their client on the stand. And she says, "Well I told that cop this, and I told him I was going to call my attorney, and . . ." Then that defense attorney is going to call that cop back on the stand. "Did you hear what she just said? Yeah. Is that true? Well, I remember her saying all that. Is it in your report? Why not? What stuff do you decide to leave out? What stuff do you decide to put in?" The facts

are the defendant is going to say whatever she wants and the cop isn't going to be quite sure.

The prosecutor is well aware of the specific rules of discovery and court procedure. He needs a police report that addresses his concerns and the exact situation for which it will be used. This particular report perplexes the prosecutor, and he identifies all the issues that could arise in the future. He is completely bound to only the details reported by the officer. This constrains his subsequent investigation (that is, he cannot interview a witness he doesn't know was on the scene) and limits his ability to decide what to do with the case (that is, without knowing someone heard the female suspect say, "Don't hit me, don't hit me," the prosecutor could decide there is not enough evidence to press charges on either person involved in the dispute).

Prosecutors inevitably end up constrained by the information in the police report, while officers feel rushed to write reports quickly and return to the field to back up fellow officers on calls. Taking the "extra ten minutes" that Guston requests may seem impossible to the officer who feels compelled to return to the street and support his or her fellow officers by writing a report as quickly and efficiently as possible. Details that an officer does not feel belong in the genre (statements that aren't facts, admittance of police officer mistakes, seemingly unimportant details) end up being some of the items that the prosecutor would really like to see included.

In this scenario, the prosecutor must rely on the officer for social capital and his ability to prosecute the case. The rules of discovery dictate that although a defense attorney can bring up anything he or she wishes at trial, the prosecutor is limited to what is in the police report and what the prosecutor's investigation has found separately. All information known to the prosecutor must be turned over to the defense attorney, but of course the defense does not have the same requirement. Witnesses or information unknown to the prosecutor can be presented in court by the defense (like the witnesses that Lewis does not name in the report) and can throw the prosecutor's case into jeopardy.

Guston shared a story about another police officer, which demonstrates a lack of understanding in the way reports work in the courtroom.

> I had a veteran cop, a good cop, bring me in something the other day. A detective. No complaints, pretty thorough. It had to do with terroristic threatening. On whatever date, he received [a] text message from 1234567, that said, "You are going to get what is coming to you." Next day, "I'm going to beat your ass, going to kill you, blah blah blah." Victim says he and Joe have been fighting and having problems forever. But I have a big problem because there is nothing in there that tells me that that number belongs to Joe. All I need is a statement from the victim saying, "That is Joe's phone number. He has had that number for years." Or, "He has called me ten times from that number." But just that information: I received some texts. Joe and I have been having problems. With no "those texts came from Joe's phone," I've got to have that connection. The first defense in any of those cases is, "Well, my friend had my phone. That was my cousin. . . ." To cops I think it seems so obvious because they are on the scene, they are talking to them, it is visceral. But that's not how it is in the courtroom, you know what I mean? You have to be able to draw a line from A to B to C. If I'm a judge and someone brought that to me, I would go, "Well, this is from that number, but does it belong to Joe?" And so again, it is not necessarily that I am faulting them, their perception is it is right in front of me boom, boom, boom, A to B to C. My perception is that is not how it happens in the courtroom. We have to do this in a certain manner and have to be able to draw each little line individually.

In this situation, Guston describes a "veteran cop, a good cop" who does not understand how police reports work for prosecutors, the job that the report needs to do in connecting all of the pieces in order for prosecutors to move a case forward. In this report, even a "thorough" job of detail and information cannot supply the connection that Guston needs in order to ensure the charge of terroristic threatening. Clearly, Officer Lewis's report is not unique. My discussion with Guston includes several examples of similar reports and police officer mindsets.

It is troubling that officers may not understand how their reports are read and used by the prosecutor. The report must be able to link the evidence to a specific charge. In the case of the terroristic threatening example, the officer needed to specifically state in the report that the phone number on the text message belonged to "Joe," so the prosecutor could link the threats back to Joe. Guston is thinking about the next links in the chained literacy event, the defense attorney and the judge. He knows that in order to make a charge and be successful in court, he needs evidence to be clear and properly linked to the case. Guston notes that officers are writing down the evidence on scene, and it seems clear to them how the evidence is linked together. From a prosecutor's perspective, though, the facts are not always held together and connected in the way they need to be for the courtroom. The officer assumes that the agentive function of the report will be successful, but the prosecutor sees that it fails completely for his purposes.

I asked Guston if training could correct problems like these in reports. He responded,

> It is just a shift in mindset. . . . You are not just writing this report to refresh you on what happened. There are discovery requirements that we have to meet based upon what you put in this report. I use this report as a guide for soliciting testimony from you and witnesses and victims. So, you know, you have to look at it a little bit differently than "this is what I want to remind myself of."

Officer Lewis remarked several times that the police report document was used to help him remember the details of the event. Even Sergeant Cuddy claimed that the report is used by an officer to refresh his or her memory on the stand during trial. Officers are unaware of the high use value of these reports in helping prosecutors make critical charging decisions. Because so few officers actually end up testifying at trial, perhaps a "shift in mindset," as Guston suggests, is warranted. However, a shift in mindset must include the way in which officers and others understand the report genre itself. More training may not be the simple answer to close the gap between the officer's presentation of facts and the prosecutor's expectations. Time constraints, fear, lack of understanding of other readers and report purposes—all add to the current state of police officer writing practices. A shift in mindset will not be possible in most police department climates. Officers and supervisors want a report that makes them look good and demonstrates probable cause. Prosecutors want a report that helps them determine how to prosecute a case. It seems that these two purposes are often in competition. Both groups want the report to build their social and cultural capital; however, because the report needs to serve so many varied purposes, it is difficult for an officer to write a report that satisfies both groups, especially when officers are not clear in their writing or lack the cultural capital to understand exactly how prosecutors use their reports and for what purpose.

Guston argued that officers should not try to justify their own actions in reports. He noted,

> You don't have to fluff. . . . If your report is written objectively, there is nothing for the defense attorney to pick on you. If you are trying to bolster, "Well, she was very agitated and he was quite da da da," I don't want to hear that shit. I don't need extra adjectives. I don't need it. I mean, "He was upset. She was agitated. She was bleeding." Not bleeding "profusely"! Take a picture. I will determine if it was profusely or not.

Guston challenges the position of power an officer assumes when adding subjective information in a report. He argues that instead of trying to improve or "bolster" the report with adjectives and conclusions, officers should stick to the simple objective facts of what they observed. His assertion that he, as prosecutor, will make the determination on what is "profusely or not" suggests that officers are supposed to be mere recorders of all available information on scene, while prosecutors, by contrast, decide what that information actually means. In this scenario, officers are not allowed interpretation in their reports, even though their actual role as police officers requires constant interpretation of events and determination of what to do next in emotionally charged and dangerous situations. If prosecutors expect no deductive reasoning in police reports, then officers are being asked to use this kind of reasoning in one part of their job, but not in the other. This is not only confusing, but in direct conflict with what officers think should be in reports. The use value for officers is not in making charging decisions or upholding a prosecutor's reputation, but in securing their own status as a good officer and in reminding themselves of what happened on scene. Thus, they make their own determination when writing the report: what they want to be reminded of, and what is important for future recall. Report writing is an *act* of deductive reasoning—this is important, that is not important.

AGENCY, READERS, AND THE REPORT GENRE

At the end of our interview, I asked Guston what he would do with the case now that he had read the report. He stated,

> Umm, I will have to wait and see. . . . It is a problem. I can't imagine a cop not realizing witness information is important. I mean people have gone to the gas chamber on witness testimony . . . He has got to remember if he works ten cases a month and there are sixty cops over there, that means I have 600 cases. So I'm sorry if it takes him five more minutes to say where the location of the wasp spray is. Put it in the report. I have to look at this report and witness statements. That is all I have to go on when I decide to plea or take it to trial. I can't sit down and look at every single thing, watch all the videos, and everything else to make decisions on that many cases a month. It is just impossible. So what I need is the cop to tell me everything I need to know in that report. And they should know what I need to know. And, you know, the reality is they don't.

The prosecutor expects a report to provide him with a summary of the evidence that he can use in order to facilitate his decision to prosecute. These documents are so important because they must provide the agency the prosecutor needs to go up the chain and make the charge. Guston expects the report to be thorough, including every detail he needs and connecting the evidence so that he can make a correct charge in the case. But he admits that, in reality, officers don't know what the prosecutor needs to know. Although Guston wants every detail put in the report because he doesn't have time to review the evidence from every case, the reality is that an a-rhetorical report is impossible to create.

In one of her research projects, Devitt was charged with rewriting jury instructions so they could be understood by jury members while also satisfying the trial lawyers' requirements. She notes that "no matter how much I elaborated, no matter how many assumptions I made explicit, I could not capture in those instructions all the information that the lawyers considered relevant to the jury's task" (Devitt, Bawarshi, and Reiff 545). Devitt's experience is similar to what police officers are asked to do in report writing. They must take all observable data, witness statements, suspect/victim statements, and interview responses and create a report that serves not only their own purposes but those of their supervisor and department, prosecution office, defense, and judge. It is incongruous to think that officers (who aren't experts in the field of writing, rhetoric, and genre) would be able to provide a report that always satisfied prosecutors and defense attorneys when Devitt herself was unable to do so.

The differing purposes and requirements at play in these situations are just too distinct to have one document satisfy all of them. And the truth is that officers always make judgments about what to include and what to leave out of police reports. Their reasoning may seem flawed to prosecutors or others, but, as in the case of Officer Lewis, officers have very specific reasoning for what they include and what they do not. Brand reminds us, "Writing . . . is an exercise in inclusion and exclusion, a lesson in decision making and choice" (437). All summary, all documentation, all reports of various kinds require the writer to make decisions about what to include and what to leave behind. Police reports, because they have so many readers who use the document for their own purposes, are remarkably difficult to write. Even veteran officers who are praised for their reports might be criticized if prosecutors and others in the court system knew what had been left out.

In addition, affect is completely ignored in the training of police report writing, yet it must be a part of the writing and selection of facts to include framing, context, and so on. To ignore the fact that officers are human beings, who will undeniably make decisions based on their own interpretations, emotions, perceptions, and understandings, is a problem. Everyone in the chained literacy event of a police report needs to comprehend what is going on and what is at stake at each link in the chain. Police officers are not robots, and prosecutors are not detectives. These two groups have vastly different notions of who should be empowered by the police report genre. What agency does this genre have for these players? What kinds of work does the report do in different contexts? How do the answers to these questions demonstrate the power working in these literacy chains?

THE ISSUE OF PURPOSE

The instrumental value, that is, the work that is expected of these reports, is often underestimated by the police officer, supervisor, and prosecutor. The prosecutor expects police reports to help him or her make charging decisions, plea agreements, and initial investigations, while the officer and supervisor use the document to support institutional memory and reputation. The document needs to work, and work well, for each group concerned, but it seems that officers don't always write reports that are useful for the prosecutor. In turn, documents that officers craft in order to help their reputations as qualified officers can backfire and expose their weaknesses. This paradox of a good report becoming a poor one based on the various purposes the genre supports is evidence of the contested space in which a police report functions. In the quotation that opened this chapter, Winsor argues that genres are a "resource that can be deployed, manipulated, contested, and regulated" (11). The officer, supervisor, and prosecutor are all in some way contesting and regulating the police report genre for their own purposes and means.

However, it isn't the case that officers are being willfully dis-
obedient or manipulative regarding the requests of the prosecutor.
Guston came to the realization in our interview that officers just
don't know what he needs in a police report. His last comment
to me recognized that while he thinks officers should know what
he requires in a police report, the reality is that they don't. Officer
Lewis had none of the concerns that troubled Guston. Lewis felt he
was doing a good and thorough report by saying that photos were
taken. He knew that this would be important information for the
prosecutor and others. He didn't realize that Guston couldn't go to
evidence and look at the photos for every case needing his review.
Similarly, Lewis assumed that the prosecutor could easily find the
witnesses by interviewing the parties involved in the disturbance.
If at that time the witnesses had agreed to cooperate, their statements could have been taken into evidence. By not including the
statements or witness information, Lewis did not provide enough
information for the prosecutor to act on. The lack of details and
witness statements turned a promising case, or at least one that
wasn't just a he said/she said, into a more complicated puzzle. The
officer managed to create a useful document for himself, but not a
useful one for his reader, the prosecutor.

In my interview with Dan Hausz, a district attorney in Arkansas, he stated that police reports are what "drives the office of the
prosecutor." Their value is so great that he added, "I can't really
emphasize enough the importance of this document." This sense
of importance is reflected in the complicated nature of the genre, a
genre that could add value for multiple purposes and audiences, but
also a genre that has the effect of constructing power for some and
diminishing power for others. Referring to Winsor again, genres
are "a way in which power is constructed, organized, and put into
effect" (11). Hausz and Guston understand the agentive effect a
report can possess. They need this effect to work for them. Hausz's
main complaint, similar to Guston's, was that "police reports don't
always reflect all an officer does." He explained that many times the
names of witnesses, and other officers' names who collected various evidence, addresses, and phone numbers, were not written in

the report. These "little" details are the ones that become critically important.

ADVOCACY IN REPORTS

It is one thing for lawyers to believe that officers are unintentionally leaving out important information, but it is another if prosecutors believe that officers are advocating for their own actions. If, for example, an officer leaves out witness statements that contradict or complicate a situation in which the officer decides to make an arrest, the prosecutor will not give much value or credence to that officer's portrayal of facts and the narratives of events. Because prosecutors may deem reports subjective, rather than objective, they criticize officers for not writing reports that have cultural and social capital for the prosecutorial office—that is, reports that provide the prosecutor with the knowledge he or she needs and maintain his or her reputation as a good prosecutor. Prosecutors lose social capital when they are unable to close cases and produce positive outcomes. Guston highlights this reality when he says that he will "look like a dumbass" if certain details are left out of police reports. He doesn't wish to be embarrassed in court and in front of other lawyers. He has his own reputation to uphold. As he notes, he can't go around "null processing domestic assaults," or the public-at-large will start to ask about the kind of job he is doing.

The lack of details or critical information in reports can also have real consequences for the judicial system as a whole. Hausz claimed in our interview that his office spent a lot of time "tracking down witnesses, speaking with officers for clarification, and looking for supporting documents." When I pressed him for how many work hours go into such searches, he couldn't quantify it but did say it was "significant." This means that real dollars and resources are being spent around the country in local and state prosecuting offices filling in the blanks left by officers. The number of suppression hearings, in which defense attorneys try to get cases dismissed by a judge on technicalities, could be greatly reduced, according to Hausz, if officers would include details about reading Miranda rights or mention video of police stops in the report. These are often the things left out of reports that defense attorneys use to try to get a case dismissed. Judicial efficiency, court time, and unknown amounts of human resources go into reading and sorting out police report information.

Micro-Chapter

The Game

OFFICER JOHN SEAWRIGHT ARRIVED AT THE COURTHOUSE and could not help but notice the large number of people in the courtroom. It was arraignment day for the county jail, and fifty or so men and women were waiting their turn before the judge. John had been called to testify in a suppression hearing on a domestic violence case. Counselor Laffoon, the defense attorney for the case, had filed a motion to suppress the evidence officers acquired from a consensual search of a home and vehicle.

John remembered well the night of the domestic dispute. He and his supervisor arrived on the scene and found a woman visibly distraught. She revealed that after a verbal fight, her husband had taken out his gun and unloaded the bullets from the magazine. He had then taken one of the bullets and pushed it into her forehead, telling her, "This is what it's going to feel like when this bullet goes through your head."

Upon hearing her story, the officers asked for consent to search the home and find the weapon. The woman gave them consent to enter; however, her husband refused to let the officers inside the home. John and his supervisor discussed the situation onsite and agreed they should enter the home based solely on the wife's consent. John told his supervisor, "Even if the evidence gets thrown out in court, I can remove a gun from inside a home where a domestic situation has just occurred and keep everyone safe for the night."

Once the officers were inside the home, the woman told John that she thought her husband had put the gun in his car, which was parked inside the garage. This statement was a critical point in the case. Because the car was inside the home (in the garage), the woman's initial consent to enter and search the home allowed the officers to also search the car, as it was "inside" the residence at that time. John asked for consent to search the car, even though this was already legally allowed, and the woman agreed. Inside the car console, he found the weapon, magazine, and bullets. The man was arrested for Domestic Assault and Terroristic Threatening and taken to the county jail for the night.

At the suppression hearing, Counselor Laffoon argued that because the man did not give consent to search his home, everything recovered for evidence from the home that night should not be allowed in trial. John was called to the stand to testify.

Counselor Laffoon walked John through the night in question. "Now, Officer Seawright, when you arrived, you entered the home and went straight to the garage, correct?"

John answered, "No, I first asked for consent to enter the home."

"And then you went directly to the garage and searched the car," Laffoon interrupted.

"No. First, I searched the house for the gun." John explained, "The woman then told me she thought maybe the gun was in his car."

"And then you went directly to the car and began your search, ignoring my client's request that you not search the vehicle," Laffoon said.

John looked at Counselor Laffoon and then at his client. John continued, "I asked the woman for consent to search the car prior to searching the vehicle. The defendant did not say anything to me about the car. In fact, once I went to the garage, he stopped talking altogether."

During this testimony, Laffoon tried several times to stop and confuse John by skipping a step or changing the order of the steps as he reviewed what had happened that night. At each misrepresentation of his actions, John stopped Laffoon and corrected him, going over the true order of events from the evening. Laffoon eventually thanked John, and the judge dismissed him. John looked out at the courtroom of people and stepped down from the stand.

The judge in the case denied the motion to suppress the consensual search of the home and the evidence found within it. He noted that because the man and woman were married and they shared ownership of the home in the eyes of the law, the woman could grant entry with or without the approval of the man. The next day at his trial, the man pled guilty to domestic assault and was sentenced to thirty days in jail.

A short time after this case, Counselor Laffoon was elected circuit court judge. The next time John saw Judge Laffoon in court, he asked the judge if he remembered the case. Laffoon responded, "Yes, I do. You did very well that day. You were very professional." John laughed and thanked him for saying so.

↬

The defense attorney was tasked with helping his client stay out of jail. He attempted to do this by finding a weakness in the police report and capitalizing on it. John and his supervisor knew that their call to enter the house and take the gun could be questioned in court; however, both agreed that it was better to remove the gun and apologize later than to come back to the house that night for a suicide or homicide. The officer clearly had consent to enter the home from one of the home's residents, and he obtained an additional consent to search the vehicle located inside the garage. Laffoon hoped that he could get the officer to make a mistake on the stand, which in turn would help his client. It didn't work, but John and Laffoon both understood that this was the game that had to be played. John had to defend what he had done that night, even though it was clearly legal, appropriate, and in the couple's best interest, and the attorney had to do everything he could to produce doubt about the way consent was granted in order to defend his client.

4

Police Reporting and Public Trust

> They compose in environments that are shot through with competing interests, rival owners, and contentious ideas about the value and status of their writing.
>
> —Brandt, "When People Write" 171

OFFICERS ARE NOT ALWAYS SEEN AS TRUSTWORTHY agents with credible authority. The court of public opinion often cross-examines the training, motives, character, abilities, and actions of police officers. Likewise, defense attorneys frequently question officers on these very same issues in order to create doubt about officers' recollection and interpretation of events. An officer's report is rarely taken at face value by anyone other than the officer. The other readers in the chained literacy event are looking for mistakes, missing information, links to evidence, and officer misconduct. Nowhere is this more true than in the reading done by the defense attorney.

Once the prosecutor has read a report and decided to file charges, the suspects are given a court date when they can plead guilty, innocent, or in some instances, no contest. For suspects who plead innocent, another court date is set for trial. At the first court date and all subsequent dates, suspects can have a defense attorney present to aid in their defense. Chris Allen is a defense attorney who works with clients facing charges in Jackson District Court.[1] He has been in private practice for several years and is a partner at his firm. He worked in a prosecutor's office prior to becoming a defense attorney, so he has seen both sides of case law and the interpretation of police reports.

I met with Allen in his office, located in a town near Jackson. The area was in a recently rejuvenated downtown district bustling with restaurants, high-end boutiques, and specialty stores. His firm's building was unassuming but well placed on the trendy street. The receptionist asked me to wait in the well-appointed lobby while she rang Allen in his office. He greeted me warmly and showed me into his office, a cozy room with modern furniture and a large desk. We exchanged pleasantries and engaged in a casual conversation before getting to the police report analysis.

CIVIL LIBERTIES AND REPORT WRITING

I slid the report across the desk and asked Allen to read it and tell me what he saw as problems or opportunities for the defense in the report. He began by reading the narrative completely and then looked through the suspects' written statements, affidavits, and other attached documents. He looked up at me and complained that this report was similar to all the others that he has read. He argued,

> Just from reading these, and it is pretty much the same with all of them, most of these are typically cut and paste in some form or fashion. So, umm, you know the first sentence says, "The officer responded to the residence reference a disturbance." I would want to know, and I think even the prosecutor would want to know, well, he responded but why did he respond? Who called? Was it anonymous? Was it someone with actual knowledge? Was it somebody three doors down that heard a noise? Was it the right house? How does he know?

Right away, Allen was looking for more detailed information in the report. He did not read past the first sentence before he saw the need for more clarification. For him, it is not enough to note that dispatch sent the officer to an address. He wants to know the circumstances surrounding the call—the information Officer Lewis and I had as we approached the scene (see Chapter 1). This context could be very important for the defense in creating a plausible and credible case. It would aid Allen in deciding how serious the dispute might have been at the time of dispatch and how concerned the officers might have been when they arrived. For example, if someone three doors down from the house had called the police because she heard a woman screaming for her life, Allen could infer that the domestic dispute was alarming neighbors and could have been serious and potentially violent. In this type of call, he could expect officers to forgo typical procedures like knocking and asking for permission to enter (civil rights liberties) because if someone's life is in danger, police are allowed to enter a home in order to prevent a likely injury or death. Because Allen was not sure of the context of the call or what Officer Lewis was told by dispatch, he could not ascertain what Lewis was legally allowed or not allowed to do on arrival. This uncertainty continued throughout his assessment of the report.

> And so he says, "He was met at the door." Well, that doesn't make a whole lot of sense. Did he knock on the door? Was she standing there waiting? How did that come about? Did he knock on the door and she had to come out right then? And so did he even have authority, is I guess the word I will use, to be there? Was he inside the threshold, was he not? And then he goes right into "I met her at the door," which sounds like perhaps a consensual encounter, to speaking with her. It's just—we need to know how he got in the house. The State needs to know. I need to know. Either one of these people has the right to refuse consent, and since it is a residence, it has to be written consent. So there is a big gap there to me.

Allen is referring to constitutional rights provided for in the Fourth Amendment to the US Constitution. This amendment assures the people of their right to be "secure in their persons, houses, papers, and effects, against unreasonable searches and seizures." The amendment secures these rights by requiring "probable cause, supported by oath or affirmation," as the only way that this right could legally be suspended. Allen addresses a Fourth Amendment question here when he ponders whether Officer Lewis has the right to enter the house and to speak with the parties therein. A sworn warrant from a judge is typically required to enter a home unless consent has been given. Allen believes only "written" consent in this case would be appropriate because he doesn't have proof (via the police report) that the officer felt he could violate Fourth Amendment rights because someone's life was in danger.

Allen, still reading from the first paragraph, noted,

> And so then he goes into this conversation, and the initial lady he spoke with says it is an "abusive relationship." I would love to know what that actual conversation was that he summed up with, "well, it is abusive." That [the conversation/interview between Officer Lewis and this woman] is obviously completely left out. And again, throughout all of this, unless I am missing it, we don't see where they are at. We don't know where they are at, and there was no altercation going on when he [Officer Lewis] got there. Umm, so it is not a great report, but, candidly, I haven't seen many great reports.

Allen repeats his concern that the officer may not have had the right to be in the home and questioning these people. This is important because if the defense could prove that the officer didn't have the right to be in the home or interviewing these parties, then the resulting arrests could be declared unjust or unwarranted, and the case dismissed. For the defense, details such as those revolving around constitutional rights are critical in crafting a case and defending clients. These details will be difficult to prove because there is nothing in the report addressing them. Even though I was on scene that night, I don't remember whether Officer Lewis asked to enter the home and then asked for consent to talk to the people present. The fight was over, and both people seemed eager to tell their side of the story, with the exception of the witnesses who did not wish to write formal witness statements.

At trial, the constitutional concern would be a practical one for the defense to raise, but the officer could claim that he asked for consent and it was granted. The judge would then have to determine if this was true, or if consent was actually needed. Of course, if the officer had simply put in the report that he asked for consent and it was given, or that he didn't need consent because the quarrel was ongoing and he had to protect citizens from injury or death, then this mystery would be a moot point. A document attached to the report providing written consent, as many officers in Jackson require for vehicle searches, would have resolved the issue entirely.

REPRESENTATION AND AUTHORITY IN THE REPORT

After Allen completed reading the report, I asked him if he would represent either of the parties.

He replied,

I would represent either one of these people, and I don't think the State would be able to prove anything on these particular charges. But, you know ideally with reports like these, it would be wonderful if there was a body mic on recording so you could compare it and see what the actual conversation was.

Allen is concerned about the lack of conversational evidence in the report. Officer Lewis determines the relationship is "abusive" but does not write how he determined this or what the woman said to him regarding the nature of the relationship. The prosecutor also questioned how Officer Lewis determined the relationship was "abusive," and even went so far as to argue that how a person qualifies a relationship, and the pronouns he or she uses, is an important factor in these types of events. The determination of the relationship as abusive wasn't Lewis's own conclusion. As I discovered while sitting with Officer Lewis when he wrote the report, he simply used the woman's written statement for his description of what happened. She claimed the relationship was abusive, so that is how he described it in the report. The fact that much of the written report comes from the woman's written statement, and not from an actual conversation she had with Officer Lewis, is unclear to readers of the report.

Despite the fact that Lewis interviewed the woman and others on the scene, he relied on the written statements to determine what to include in the report and what to leave out. This hurts his ethos with both the defense attorney and the prosecutor, because neither sees him as credibly reporting the conversations he had with those arrested and the witnesses on scene. Both the prosecutor and the defense question Lewis's conclusion, and once they question the conclusion, they begin to question other statements presented as facts in the report. This domino effect hurts Officer Lewis's cultural (competence) and social (reputation) capital. The report invites criticism once one mistake is found, and the officer loses authority in the way he would like others to view the events of that evening.

I told Allen that I was on scene during the questioning of the individuals, and that there were two witnesses on the scene as well. I asked him if he would be interested in knowing more about the witnesses in the report. He replied,

> Absolutely! Because they are likely people who may not have any skin in the game, so to speak, so I want to know what they heard. Unfortunately, that happens a lot where there are other people present, and it may help or hurt your case as a defense attorney, but they aren't mentioned. No idea why. Did he even take any statements from them?

Allen notes again that this report is similar to others he sees on a regular basis. He seems to welcome the idea of witness statements and witness testimony and wonders why officers leave these witnesses out of reports. Similar to the prosecutor, Allen believes that witnesses may be people who would be more honest because they have little at stake, like jail time. They can present a perspective that helps clarify what the arrested parties claim. As Prosecutor Guston mentioned, it "takes it from being a he said/she said."

Allen also claims that witnesses being left out of reports "happens a lot." This is troubling. Why are officers failing to include details, testimony, and conclusions of witnesses? Is it because they feel the witnesses' observations aren't needed and would take too much time to include?[2] Do the witnesses merely corroborate the officer's story and thus are deemed unimportant? Or is the exclusion something more? A need to provide only one viewpoint with an aim to minimize other viewpoints? It may be what Foucault calls "rarefaction," the authoritative practice that legitimizes some speakers and delegitimizes others so that certain speakers can be excluded from various discourses (346–58). Although Officer Lewis may not be consciously aware of the power and privilege he has in determining who is included in and who stays outside of the police report discourse, the impact of this symbolic power cannot be underestimated. The silencing of people, events, details, and circumstances is not a police practice that the public or legal system can endorse. Actions like this could easily support misogynistic or racist ideologies. Officer biases, known or unknown to the officers themselves, could be driving what ends up in police reports and what is left out. Whether careless or innocent, the exclusion of facts is not harmless.

I explained to Allen that the witnesses didn't want to make written statements, but that one or both had claimed to hear the woman screaming, "Don't hit me. Don't hit me." Allen replied, "Well, he didn't bother with it [including the statement "Don't hit me"] because it helped to enforce what he already knew was going to be his action. . . . 'I have decided you are both going to jail.' So yeah, that is completely left out." Allen assumes that Officer Lewis intentionally left out the witness's statement about hearing the woman screaming "Don't hit me. Don't hit me" because it does not corroborate his story. Lewis knows that he arrested both parties, and he does not want to call attention to evidence that suggests the woman might be the victim in the disturbance. He chose to not complicate the narrative of his report with details that did not help build the story he was creating. Kahneman claims, "It is the consistency of the information that matters for a good story, not its completeness" (87). The officer leaves out the witness's verbal statement because it doesn't aid the story's cohesion. It creates doubt, conflict, and suspicion in the officer's narrative of events.

Allen doesn't call Lewis's decision to leave out the witness's story unethical, but the fact that the inclusion of the statement "Don't hit me. Don't hit me" doesn't fit nicely into the narrative Lewis creates suggests a problem with his choice to leave it out. Unlike the prosecutor, however, Allen is not upset or surprised by the officer's report. He sees problems in the report and in the officer's interpretation of the situation, but he sees these inaccuracies as opportunities for defending a client, not as stumbling blocks to successful prosecution.

POLICE REPORTS ARE RHETORICAL DOCUMENTS

During our interview, Allen argued that officers don't understand how their assumptions and advocacy become "facts" in the report. He noted,

> Another really interesting thing is they get in this habit of "because I see this then it must be true." It is like a self-fulfilling prophecy. She mentions wasp spray, so he says there is wasp spray on the bed. Well, that is interesting that he knows that is wasp spray on the bed. I don't know how he knows that is wasp spray. It could be water. It could be anything else. But you know, then "Michael had red watery eyes from the wasp spray." Well, maybe he was drunk. Maybe he was high. It should be that he had "red watery eyes." It should be the things that he observed, all of the things that he observed. But now in here, he has this conclusion and unfortunately it goes on to become one of those conclusions that becomes a fact in testimony. But we don't know why he had red watery eyes. We don't know if it was wasp spray on the bed as well as the walls. We just know something was there. So, it is not a great report.

Officers may fall into a routine of what Kahneman calls "WYSI-ATI," which is the acronym for "what you see is all there is" (86). The problem with WYSIATI is that it leads to biases, overconfidence, neglect of other alternatives, and incorrect framing of events. The human brain is made to think fast in many situations, which often results in incorrect or misguided conclusions (87–88). Officers need to fight against this natural predisposition in order to consider other possibilities before reaching fast conclusions. In high-pressure and often dangerous situations, this may be incredibly difficult. It is another example of the complicated environments in which officers navigate events in order to create reports that work for many different audiences and purposes.

Both Allen and the prosecutor want an objective report without officer conclusions or subjective detail. Even if the evidence doesn't side with his client, Allen wants to see all the objective facts rather than conclusions and summaries made by the officer. The prosecutor noted in his interview that he wanted only objective fact as well, and he urged officers to stop using adjectives and advocacy in their reports. I believe both men feel that police officers use their agency and power to reveal those facts that support the story they want to create and to exclude evidence that doesn't support that story. If this is true, it is disturbing and suggests that officers are not always trusted by the very men and women who rely on their police reports to make critical decisions in the criminal justice system.

However, are the expectations of prosecutors and defense attorneys actually achievable? The police report is a rhetorical document with an argument at its core. The officer is tasked with describing an event, but there is much more going on than listing objective data from the scene. Officers must prove probable cause and link the evidence provided to a criminal charge. As far as I can determine, linking evidence to state statutes in order to justify or prove probable cause for an arrest represents an argument. Despite prosecutor and defense demands that a police report not include summaries and conclusions of information, an argument must be made in order for officers to meet the requirements of the genre.

Officers may think they need to advocate or defend their actions on scene because of the current police and public climate. Officers who feel they are under attack, or at least under a critical eye, might feel more pressure to prove themselves in their reports.

As an illustration, let us examine the recent shooting of an unarmed citizen by a police officer. Officer Darren Wilson shot and killed Michael Brown, an unarmed African American man, on August 19, 2014, in Ferguson, Missouri. According to the Department of Justice report, minutes later "residents began pouring onto the streets," and officers were threatened verbally by the crowd (8). The incident triggered a week of protests in Ferguson, some resulting in violence and looting. The document that many were waiting for, the police report, never surfaced (Winter). Although a report detailing Brown's theft of cigarillos from a convenience store shortly before his death was made public a few days after the shooting, an incident report on the shooting death of Brown was never filed.

Ferguson police claim this is because the matter was turned over to the St. Louis County Police Department on the day of the incident, and any report should be made by that organization (Winter). Notably, the public outcry and media coverage of events in Ferguson created an environment that would test any police department and subsequent investigation team, but the lack of a police report about the shooting further angered citizens around the country and increased public distrust of the police department.

Allen recounted a recent conversation he'd had with a prosecutor in an Oklahoma county regarding police reports. It is a dire statement about police report writing and the possible future for police departments. Allen recalled,

> I talked to their prosecutor, and she told me point blank she had asked her officers to quit writing reports. [Allen is talking about officers filing reports without narratives of the event. Officers send an almost blank report to the prosecutor, listing only names and charges.] Because their reports were so bad, they were being flipped around, and the reports at the end of the day ended up helping the defense case more than the State trying to prosecute them. So, um, I don't think that the State really likes reports. I think that they are a necessary evil because otherwise they [officers] are not going to be able to testify about date, time, that kind of stuff.

It is shocking that a prosecutor asked officers to quit writing reports because the reports were so poor. But is this really the solution to poor report writing? Allen claims that the State considers reports "a necessary evil." The officers need reports in order to provide a mnemonic when called to testify months after an arrest, but reports can be so poorly written that they actually hurt the prosecutor's case rather than help it. Ceasing to write reports hardly seems like a viable solution. Given the current state of affairs for police and public relations in the United States, the opposite should actually be the case. Police departments need more comprehensive reporting than ever before. The problems innately tied to the police report genre must be addressed before future efforts at improving police reports can be successful.

ADVOCATING IS NOT THE ANSWER

Despite an officer's attempt to advocate for a decision in the police report, this attempt often fails and results in less ethos and authority. Allen complained,

> It makes absolutely no sense that he takes two people to jail, and there are two people there that weren't in the altercation, and he isn't going to include what they said. It makes zero sense. None whatsoever. . . . It kind of looks like a report that was written by an officer that was just annoyed to be there, if that makes sense. "Sprayed me with wasp spray." "Was throwing things around the room." It really is just a bad report. It is. They should be all-inclusive.

As a person who was with the officer when he was on scene and when he was writing the report, I did not detect a hint of apathy, disregard, or carelessness in his manner, yet the prosecutor and defense attorney seem to believe he is apathetic, or unethical, or both. In contrast, I think the officer lacks awareness and understanding of the choices he is making in the report and what these choices do to his ethos. He is completely unaware of how the prosecutor and defense might view the lack of witness information or detailed conversations between the suspects and himself. Officer Lewis lacks a comprehensive view of the criminal justice system and this report's place in it. He mentioned himself as the main reader of the document so many times that he must believe other readers need the same information he needs. The interviews with readers in the chained literacy event show the inaccuracy of his assumptions about what to include in the report and why. Beyond this lack of awareness and understanding, though, are the nearly impossible demands of the genre, a genre that requires so much for so many that it becomes ineffective for everyone.

I asked Allen if the report gave him some ammunition to use as a defense attorney. Officers would, obviously, try to prevent having holes in their reports that could aid a defense attorney, and this is something that Lewis was clearly trying to avoid, as I observed during our interview. Allen responded,

Oh absolutely. It isn't like calling an officer to the stand and calling him "liar, liar." That is not effective. But what is effective, is close calls like this when you go through with the officer about his training, and the academy. Did they teach you to write a report? What do you include in that report? Don't you think it is important to include all the details? Yada yada yada. And then you bring out, well, why didn't you include that Joe Smith was there? Don't you think that is important? Jane Doe? What about this? What about that? Why don't you have these things in your report? So, you get to that point [where] it doesn't necessarily tear their credibility down, but it certainly makes a judge or jury look at them differently. It helps from the defense side, absolutely.

Similar to the prosecutor, Allen calls on this officer's training to discredit his actions. He intimates in the interview what he would do if he had Officer Lewis on the stand and wanted the jury or judge to question the officer's credibility. Officer Lewis had no intention of writing a report that would irritate the prosecutor and give ammunition to the defense, but his report does just that. His ethos is harmed by the lack of concrete details regarding conversations that should be documented in the report. Likewise, Officer Lewis mentions that he was met at the door by someone (a witness), but he never recounts what that person said or how others can contact him or her. Perhaps Lewis's greatest failing is his belief that all of the report readers only need to know what he writes down. He doesn't envision the way that the prosecutor and defense attorney will question each statement and want more detailed, objective information.

Allen concluded,

If you just put it all in here, put the witnesses, put what they said, and just let it see where it falls. It is really not up to the officer to decide what is relevant or not. Put every single thing that happens. Put everyone that was there. Every witness. And if he isn't even going to put in here the witness names and what they said, even without a written statement, it makes it look like there is something to hide.

Allen sees many problems in this report, all problems that would help a potential defense. The lack of witness information; the lack of details about the call the officer was responding to; questions about how the officer obtained consent to enter the home and speak with all of these individuals; and questions about the assumptions and conclusions the officer made in his report—all these provide ample opportunities for the defense to attack the credibility of the arrests and the officer. These weaknesses are exactly what Officer Lewis tried to avoid in writing this report. However, requiring officers to write what Allen is asking for seems impossible. Even with audio and video recordings supplementing police reports, it is difficult to fully understand everything that is happening and all of the witness testimony, and to put every objective fact into a written document.

There are several reasons that officers cannot accurately complete workplace documents. One of these reasons is the need to, as Officer Lewis claimed, CYA. This sentiment is found in the workplace writing practices of other groups as well. Belfiore and colleagues find that workers and supervisors in manufacturing avoid paperwork not because they lack the basic skills necessary to complete it, but because the paperwork asks them to document their mistakes or others' (25). Similarly, Ornatowski claims that in the documents they create, writers must choose between protecting their employers or themselves, and protecting others. He argues that two incompatible goals are held out for a writer: (1) to serve the interests that employ her effectively and efficiently, while (2) being objective, plain, factual, and so on. What she finds in practice is that serving specific interests (any interests, even the most public-spirited) requires at least a degree of rhetorical savvy, and that doing so is incompatible with "objectivity," "plainness," or "clarity" (313). This is exactly the dilemma that police officers find in report writing. Officers do not want to reveal a mistake they made in the questioning of suspects, victims, and witnesses or in the processing of evidence. Likewise, they resist reporting mistakes of other officers, and as Ornatowski argues, their writing requires rhetorical devices. A police report is never a listing of facts. It is always created through the officer's lens.

BUILDING THE DEFENSE

Devitt, Bawarshi, and Reiff remind us that "the communal agendas of those who create genres may conflict with the interests of those who use them" (549). Police officers and police organizations are in charge of the report genre, despite the fact that they may be more constrained by it than liberated. As the creators of the generic conventions that rule police report writing, departments are ultimately responsible for the documents that are created. The genre (and reader) demands a type of writing that is quite impossible to produce. Police reports should be entirely objective, relevant, factual, chronological, and well written. At the same time, officers writing in this genre rarely, if ever, admit to making mistakes, admit to not understanding how an event unfolded, or acknowledge doubt about the actions they took on scene. The genre also largely excludes emotive responses or officer affect. So report writing is a difficult task for officers because they are disciplined by the genre to not include certain facts, yet are disciplined for not including them via the prosecutor or defense attorney. Their fear of cross-examination is reinforced by their writing practices, which are ultimately put on trial.

The report analyzed in this book is an example of how difficult it is to meet the requirements of the genre and the criminal justice system. Officer Lewis believed he had included all of the relevant information. He didn't acknowledge or understand that relevance is different to different readers. The defense attorney wanted more information about the witnesses and considered these details incredibly relevant to the case. Officer Lewis also attempted to write an objective document, but as we have discovered, neither the prosecutor nor the defense attorney believed it to be so. Allen complained that the officer made assumptions about the wasp spray covering the bed and walls, and that he also made assumptions about the cause of the man's red eyes rather than simply stating what he observed on scene.

Allen did not believe that this report was a good one, but acknowledged that he doesn't read very many good reports. Unlike the prosecutor, who needs the document in order to create a case for prosecution, Allen needs the report to see what mistakes the officer might have made that can help his client fight a charge. He reads between the lines of the report, asking about what is left out, what is missing. The value (and cultural capital) of the report for the defense is in what is unsaid. Who is silenced in the report and why? Does the officer follow protocol and uphold civil liberties? These questions are a starting point for a plausible defense. If there are mistakes in the report, they can be used to throw out a charge and dismiss a case. Reports can also be used by the defense to buy time and create legal postponements. The county district attorney, Dan Hausz, complained that when details are left out of police reports, defense attorneys are able to call for suppression hearings in order to suppress evidence and dismiss cases. For example, to call for a suppression hearing before the judge, Allen could use his question about whether Officer Lewis had a legal right to enter the home. Allen could argue that all evidence the officer obtained inside the home and the interviews he conducted with suspects inside the home cannot be used because he never had a legal right to be there. The hearing would require the prosecutor, defense attorney, judge, and officer to all be present, as well as courtroom recorders and other staff. This is a typical way defense attorneys delay trial and seek dismissals. This hearing could have been prevented if Officer Lewis had noted in his report that he asked for and was given consent to enter the home.

Identifying where things are left out of reports allows a defense attorney to begin to question an officer's training and attention to the job. This diminishes the officer's credibility and gives the defense an opportunity to create doubt about the events as reported by the officer. Similar to the literacy events that Heath records, defense attorneys (and all of the other report readers) bring to the reading their own contexts and values. They "bring in knowledge related to the text and interpret beyond the text for their own context; in so doing, they achieve a new synthesis of information from the text and the joint experiences of community members" (201). It may be that police officers aren't recognizing *how* their reports will be read, even if they know *who* will read them.

If officers are trying to cover up facts in their written reports, then defense attorneys are a critical part of the justice system, seeking out and exposing such practices. The reports with gaps symbolize powerful weapons in an ideological battle of police versus public in this kind of scenario. Defense attorneys could use the cultural capital of poor police reports to elevate their own reputations. The ability to find fault in police reports becomes a powerful tool for defense attorneys to use and exploit. The attorneys' own cultural and social capital, wealth, and success are all determined by their ability to protect their clients from prosecution and provide them with a credible defense. The entire career of a defense attorney rests on his or her expertise in dismantling a police report, creating doubt, and denying the facts as presented by the officer and prosecution. The more successful a defense attorney is in accomplishing those things, the more successful he or she will be in reaping economic, cultural, and social capital.

5

Police Procedure, the Legal System, and Circulations of Power

> Defendants seem especially powerless in the trial genre system, for they are not even permitted to speak except in response to the lawyer's questions. In fact, their ability to choose silence may be at times their only real power.
>
> —Devitt, *Writing Genres* 60

JUDGE FRANK LAFFOON IS THE CIRCUIT COURT JUDGE FOR the Jackson Police Department and all of the police departments in the county. His is an elected office, and he had been a judge for two years prior to our interview. He asked me to meet him in the new county courtroom near the Jackson Police Department. Stripped of all the historical charm of courtrooms in bygone eras, this new venue had very little pizazz. The walls were pale blue instead of wood paneled, and can lights were used throughout the courtroom, rather than elegant chandeliers or towering windows. The gallery chairs were upholstered in blue fabric, and each chair was attached to a bar that latched it to the floor. The only charm in the building was saved for the judge's desk, appropriately made of dark, handsome wood and elevated two or three steps above the rest of the room.

A tall, middle-aged man with dark hair and light eyes, Judge Laffoon walked out of his private chamber and greeted me as I approached the bench area of the courtroom. His wide smile was infectious as he shook my hand and asked how he could help. I explained to him that I would like him to read through the police report I had brought with me and tell me his thoughts about it. He took the report and began reading immediately. Judge Laffoon was the first of the interviewees to ask if he could write on the report, and the only one of my police report audience members to make notes on it while reading. After underlining a few sentences in the police narrative, he flipped through the supporting documents and asked me, "Am I to critique this?" I explained that I would like him to tell me his concerns with the report.

He responded,

> Sure. Well, and here is the thing: as a judge I don't necessarily care whether they have the stuff in the report or not. It does make my job a lot easier though when they do a good report. And the reason why is because what happens is, although the report itself can't be entered into evidence, they can have the report there to refresh their memory.

The judge sees the first purpose of the report, then, as a mnemonic device; this is similar to the views of the officer and supervisor. Perhaps he considers this the first use of the document because he sees officers daily bring in their reports and read from them or refer to them while on the witness stand. The judge identifies the very practical use of the document as being to "refresh their memory" first. However, he quickly notes the importance of the document for other uses:

> The thing that strikes out at me first about this is he says that he meets an individual [at the door] not a part of the disturbance. We don't know who that individual is. And we don't know what that person says about what they saw. So, you know, that is the first thing that strikes me. He is not going to remember months later, and then Jackson [the prosecutor] is not going to be able to subpoena the person, and it would be nice to know who this person is and to determine if this person has some sort of motive to lie. You just don't know, and it would have been nice to have that.

Judge Laffoon has the same witness concerns as the prosecutor and defense attorney. Information about what the witnesses saw and heard is critical, and it is obviously missing from this report. He also brings up the practical subpoena solution to a witness who may or may not want to talk about what he or she saw on scene. This is what the prosecutor noted when I explained that the officer didn't want to take the witness's name and information because she refused to write a statement. The prosecutor was outraged because he could subpoena a witness if he had the information.

CREATING KNOWLEDGE THROUGH POLICE REPORTS
The judge continued,

> The next thing that jumps out at me is that he does note that she had a bruise on her lower back and a bump on her head. Here is my problem: I don't know how long it was between when he got dispatched and when he got there, but I assume it was a matter of minutes. Here is my problem with it. If you know anything about bruising, it doesn't happen just like that [snaps his fingers]. It takes a while to come out. He didn't ask, "Look, I see a bruise on your lower back. Did you get that here?" or "I notice it is blue, or red, or it's purple." I mean, if it is purple it has been there a while, but if it is red and raised, then it wouldn't be a bruise. It would be more of an abrasion. I mean, that makes me wonder. Now, the bump on her head, yeah, that happens immediately as blood comes to the head. There needs to be more discussion about the bruise and the bump on the head because I imagine the bruise would be there from another time, and he needs to ask her if it happened earlier and how much earlier.

The judge is requesting the same kind of detailed information about the injuries that Officer Lewis's supervisor, Sergeant Cuddy, requested. Despite that direct request, Lewis only added one sentence stating that the woman did not know how her injuries had occurred. The judge would like more information about these injuries, as would the prosecutor. Officer Lewis may have thought that by taking pictures and noting this fact in the report, he did not need to describe the injuries in more detail in the report. However, the supervisor, prosecutor, and judge all asked for additional information in the report about how the injuries occurred and how the injuries appeared to Officer Lewis on the scene. The injuries are important because two people were taken to jail based on the fact that physical injuries were present. The state statute for Domestic Battery 3rd Degree insists that physical injury be present and identifiable in order to charge someone with this crime. It is important to the readers in the chained literacy event that Officer Lewis substantiate his decision to arrest by adequately detailing the injuries. The use of this document as one that proves the elements of a crime and probable cause to arrest is what concerns most of the readers. This is where the real cultural capital comes from in the report—the report's ability to create knowledge about the event and connect the elements of a crime from the legal statutes to what happened between this couple on this particular night. The creation of cultural capital is important for the officer, supervisor, prosecutor, and judge because they all need the knowledge that a crime has actually been committed and two people should be held accountable. If the officer cannot create this knowledge through the creation of the report, then it is a report that serves no one well, the exception being the defense attorney.

The judge draws on his medical understanding of bruising and injury to question the officer's story (and perhaps his credibility). Clearly, the judge has an excellent grasp of medical knowledge and terminology. It may be that he is often called on to use this kind of knowledge when making judicial decisions. The officer, however, is less familiar, or at least he appears so in his police report. The report's lack of clarity on the woman's injuries is a concern for the judge because he is not sure if the woman was actually injured on that night or on a previous one. Because the man was taken to jail for her injuries, it is important that the court know exactly how she was injured on the night in question, or if she was injured at all. The judge expects the report to create the knowledge of the woman's injuries and how they occurred in order for him to make a sound judgment.

QUESTIONING POLICE PROCEDURE

Similar to the concern expressed by the defense attorney, the judge had apprehensions about the legality of the officer's conversation with the individuals on scene. He remarked,

> Oh, and then I was wondering about the Miranda concern.[1] I mean he does separate them, and he does put them in different rooms, and I understand that he was there on a disturbance call, but at some point you['ve] got to determine is this person free to leave, and the answer is no.[2] I don't think either one of them is free to leave, and if they did try to leave, he would have arrested them right there. I think of course as you know, Miranda is in custody, custodial interrogation, so number one is, "Are you in custody?" and I think clearly you are. And second is that he didn't Mirandize either the victim or the defendant because at that point he doesn't know who is who. I don't know actually about police procedure or not, but I would imagine if you go to a disturbance call, you are going to want to put them in handcuffs, and I don't think that he did . . . I mean, that is what I would think, and I would imagine that if he didn't do that, it isn't good procedure. And second of all, I still think that even if he didn't have handcuffs on them, they were still in custody at that time, and that there was no Miranda warning given there.

The judge is concerned that the civil rights of these individuals may have been violated during this incident. The issue of Miranda is complicated when officers are trying to determine on scene who is the victim and who is the suspect. As soon as it seems apparent, however, officers are expected to read the suspect his or her Miranda rights. The judge is concerned that the officer may have violated these two individuals' civil rights, a serious legal issue.

The simple inclusion of one sentence explaining that the individuals were read their Miranda rights would resolve this question. However, Officer Lewis does not know that the judge and the defense attorney are both going to have questions about his legal ability to enter the home and question the people on scene. Lewis never raises this as an issue in his interview, nor does his supervisor. Officer Lewis is unaware that the purposes he writes for (memory and self-advocacy) do not serve him well because the judge and attorneys have vastly different and, in fact, contradictory purposes for a police report. They need a report that records the people on scene (including all witnesses) and documents police procedure (including civil rights assurances). These are not the things that Officer Lewis was thinking about as he wrote his report. The chained literacy event exposes how differently the people in the chain view the report and what they need it to do.

The judge raises an interesting point about police procedure. While he admits that he isn't sure what the police procedure is in this kind of scenario, he does insist that if the officer didn't put both people in handcuffs for questioning, then "it isn't good procedure." Judge Laffoon questions not only the officer's credibility here— did he put the two in handcuffs and read them Miranda prior to questioning?—but also the procedures used by the Jackson PD. The report is not simply a mnemonic tool for officers, as the judge first concludes. It is a vehicle that allows judicial power to access an officer's use (or ~~this can be used to~~ of civil rights, and even police pr ~~argue that writing for~~ port genre has the potential for a ~~the lawyers purpose~~ are civil rights of individuals were ~~will help to "CYA" as~~ ice procedures were followed. In (~~a cop too.~~ is diminished because he did not

I told Judge Laf hat there were two witnesses on : t. I explained that the officer did not include them because neither one wanted to make a written statement. I asked the judge if that was an adequate justification. He responded,

> I don't think so, and here is why. That may very well be the point, that they don't want to get involved, but it isn't up to them whether or not they want to get involved. As an officer, I would think that you would show up and find out who is there. Were there outstanding warrants for these people? Who am I talking to? What is going on here? Then get the name

and address and identification. Let the State decide whether
to subpoena them or not. If he [Officer Lewis] says they [the
witnesses] don't want to take the time to get involved, then
why are we arresting them [the alleged suspects]?

The judge believes that police procedure alone would dictate the
acquisition of witness identification on the scene. The fact that
there is no information on the witnesses is troubling from both a
report and a police procedure standpoint. Also, the judge questions
why these two people were arrested at all. Just like the prosecutor,
he wonders why the individuals were taken to jail when a clear aggressor was not identified on the scene or in the report. As a reader,
he questions the event's legitimacy, and this damages the reputation
of Officer Lewis and the department.

Judge Laffoon looked at his notes on the police report and continued,

This is just a pet peeve of mine and, you know, it probably
doesn't matter, but here is the thing. I get kind of tired of the
State, not necessarily the officer, but the State. They seem to
want to criminalize these type[s] of events. I mean, if you are
unable to determine who the primary aggressor was, based
upon what was told, then he arrests both of them? And I
guess the thing about that is this is okay, so now they are both
guilty? Well they can't both be guilty. The likelihood of two
people just sitting there and at the same exact time exchang-
ing punches, both intending to hurt each other, is just almost
impossible. So, I guess my point is, that as a defense lawyer,
when they arrest both of them I like that because I say, "State,
you have charged both of them, and one of them is going
to have self-defense and one of them isn't. So obviously, you
don't even know. You arrested both of them." To me, that is
built-in reasonable doubt.

Even though the judge blames the State (prosecutor) and not the
officers for criminalizing these sorts of cases, the prosecutor indi-
cates that he feels the same way as the judge. Both would like to
see a report like this not become a report at all. The judge would

offer a warning and tell the parties to behave themselves. Likewise, the prosecutor insists that the officer not arrest the individuals if he isn't going to take the time to put in all the details and evidence that need to be present in the report. The prosecutor and judge have years of experience in the judicial system. To them, a case like this just adds to the quagmire of the legal system. The officer, who has only completed one year of duty, does not have the experience or training needed to comprehend the larger picture of this case. His supervisor, however, with over seventeen years of experience, is supposed to be able to make up for Officer Lewis's lack of experience. He is supposed to know and understand what the State needs, but he evidently does not. Again, this signifies the complex nature of the report-writing process, the constraints, the reactions and questions of some of the readers, and the purposes and values surrounding each reader's own needs and uses for the document.

GIVING OFFICERS A PASS

I asked the judge if he would like to see in the report that the woman in the incident was advised by her attorney to keep wasp spray by her bed for self-defense. He replied,

> I did wonder why wasp spray was in the bedroom. I mean, I did wonder that. Uh, I guess that probably would help me to show these other instances and that she was injured, and I guess if she has used it before on him and it stopped him, that would explain why there is wasp spray in the bedroom. So yeah, that would have been something I would like to see. You do have to look at it from his [the officer's] point of view, though. I don't know how many times he has been out there, and I don't know how many times other guys have been out there. To him this is probably the sixth, seventh, eighth time we have been out here, and it always ends up dismissed, and we end up going through it, and the charges get dismissed. I'm not saying it makes it right. I'm just saying I understand why it is written the way it is.

The judge presumes that Officer Lewis has a degree of apathy toward this event and the people involved. He knows that officers often see their domestic violence arrests tossed out due to reluctant witnesses or victims. He presumes that officers must get tired of seeing the same people again and again and thus don't treat these cases with care. The judge is surprisingly sympathetic toward officers in this interview. His empathy for them in this particular case, though, may be misplaced.

Officer Lewis had been a police officer for only one year, and he never said anything on scene about being at that house several times for domestic disturbance. It is my understanding that this was his first time at this house with these individuals, so he would probably not have a history with them. In addition, in all of my interactions with Lewis, I found him to be a dedicated and serious officer. He spent a lot of time with this report, and I could tell that he was really trying to write a report that would help him recall and understand the events at a later date. While he didn't recognize the gravity of leaving out witnesses and statements such as "Don't hit me," he did attempt, in my opinion, to write a report that included the details he thought would be important to the case. It is fascinating that his report and actions on scene led the judge to presume that he was apathetic toward this couple or domestic violence cases in general. This demonstrates the damage a report can do to an officer's character (social capital) and how a report can be used by those more powerful in the chain to discredit the intentions of officers.

I asked Judge Laffoon if officers needed better training in report writing. He argued, "I would have liked to have seen 'JPD has been out here eleven times or whatever it was this month.' I think if the prosecutor had seen that, he could have said, 'Well, look, we are going to do it this time, and we are going to prosecute and we are going to be done with it.'" The judge is requesting the type of information that Officer Lewis in his interview blatantly refused to include. As he was writing the report, Lewis remarked, "Do I really need to know what their past domestic history is? No. You know, when they run their numbers they will see that. And I didn't arrest them for their past domestic battery history. I arrested them for what they were doing that night." Officer Lewis has reasons for not including historical information on the couple's domestic violence, but he is unaware that this is just the kind of information that the judge wants to see. Lewis believes that an individual's record ("run their numbers") will show this past history, but the prosecutor and the judge may not have immediate access to that kind of information. Everything they need to know must be in the report.

THE LITERACY EVENT CHAIN COMES FULL CIRCLE

Judge Laffoon identifies the first use of the report as helping the officer's memory of the event when called to testify, a mnemonic function. This is also the document's main purpose according to the officer and supervisor in their interviews. Both of these individuals stated how important it was for the officer to be reminded of the details of the event for trial. Remembering the fine details of a call many months later is, in their opinion, best done through the police report. The judge agrees, and appreciates the value of the document used on the stand to help officers remember what happened many months before trial. The purpose of the document as a mnemonic tool seems quite clear to Judge Laffoon. Of course, the judge acknowledges that the report should do more than serve as a memory device for officers.

At the document's core is the power to demonstrate probable cause and record the reason, in this case, that two people were placed under arrest and went to jail. The suspension of personal freedom and movement is an incredibly powerful purpose for a document. The cultural power of the document for the judge lies in its ability to catalogue proper procedure and to document that civil liberties were not infringed upon. He has concerns about the legality of the conversation that the officer had with the two people because they may not have been read their Miranda rights. Thus, the power and agency of the document is in reassuring the court that the officer followed proper procedures and did not violate a citizen's rights. The judge wants the report to record police procedure, which will uphold the legality of the officer's actions and increase the cultural capital of the court.

The judge notes that a good report "does make my job a lot easier." In contrast to the way a report can negatively affect the prosecutor's reputation and job, the judge identifies the document as a potential resource for him if it aids the officer. He notes the way in which the cultural capital of a mnemonic for the officer can result in cultural and social capital for himself as a judge. If an officer does a good job of recreating the scene and remembering the details of a call, the judge benefits by being able to make a judgment that includes the important facts. The power circulates from the officer to the document and on to the judge in a way that is surprising. In the place where officers are often nervous and criticized, the judge views the police report as a way to circulate power to himself and result in a trial that is easier for him to arbitrate. A report that serves the purposes of the court creates symbolic capital for the system because it makes the business of deciding who is right and who is wrong easier for the judge.

However, the judge does dismiss the effectiveness of the officer in a way that is quite different from that of the prosecutor and defense lawyer. While the prosecutor assumed Officer Lewis was lazy ("I mean, if you don't care enough to put the time into doing that") and the defense assumed he was unethical ("Well, he didn't bother with it [including their statements] because it helped to enforce what he already knew was going to be his action"), the judge suggests that he is merely apathetic ("You do have to look at it from his [the officer's] point of view, though. I don't know how many times he has been out there.") He believes that Officer Lewis has seen this couple before and has had cases with them dismissed in the past, so the officer arrested both of them and wrote a poor report because he was dispassionate about this couple and the legal system as a whole. The judge dismisses the problems in the report as the result of an apathetic officer. The symbolic capital here is that the judge has the ultimate say in what the officer did or didn't do in the report and the implication of those actions. He is in a place to judge the report and the officer and to make a ruling based on what he believes happened that night. The report is an important document for him because, based on his judgment of the report, the officer, and the people in question, he uses the document to ultimately impact the lives of all involved.

THE NEED FOR OVERSIGHT

Judge Laffoon sees his job in reading the police report as that of an oversight body. The officer should be acting within the law and within the jurisdiction of the courts. The officer is only acting in a space where he has authority to arrest. Herndl and Licona remind us that officers do not create or hold authority, but rather, they occupy the space and position where authority occurs. The authors note, "Authority, like agency, exceeds the subject: it comes before and outside the subject" (142). The position of authority an officer holds when he or she puts someone under arrest and in jail is demonstrated through the vehicle of the police report genre. When Officer Lewis took two people to jail, he was acting within his authority as an officer. However, now that the judge and defense attorney have questioned the way in which he conducted his investigation and interviews, they may determine that Officer Lewis did not have the authority to arrest two people that night. His authority as an agent of the law is awarded to him by the court and his department. The position of authority can quickly disappear as the readers in this literacy chain question his actions.

Given the current public mistrust of law enforcement, oversight seems a particularly relevant topic regarding police actions and reporting. Police officers may currently see oversight as a constraint or a criticism. If the courts and prosecutors could work with law enforcement to demonstrate how the police report genre is used to ensure police procedures are followed, perhaps officers could better mesh the multiple purposes and audiences of the genre while writing reports. It is no simple task to incorporate the varying needs of so many, but with cultural and social capital at stake, it is worth the risk for officers to examine their current practices. Ethical officers may be unintentionally leaving out information they don't realize they should include. But unethical officers may be subverting the system and hiding information that would change readers' perception if it came to light; of course this cannot be condoned, nor can we have a genre (which police control) that results in less justice rather than more.

Oversight from within the system and outside of it may be a solution in helping to solve the strained relationship between the public and the police. This is especially true for defendants who, as Devitt explains in the quotation that opened this chapter, often find themselves powerless in the courtroom. Their own silence is sometimes the most powerful agency they have. When so many grabs at authority happen in the courtroom scenario, it is critical to understand how cultural, social, and symbolic capital circulate through the police report genre.

Micro-Chapter

Hands Up

THE CALL CAME IN AT 6:05 A.M. OFFICER JOHN SEAWRIGHT had just been released from his night shift at the Jackson Police Department and was on his way home in his police cruiser. The officers starting the day shift had arrived at the station and were in the briefing room for the daily pre-shift meeting. John had not yet turned off his radio, so he heard the call come in.

The dispatcher announced, "We have a domestic violence disturbance in progress. Need immediate response to 317 W. Elm." John was two streets away. Knowing how quickly domestic violence calls could get out of hand, he responded to dispatch, "This is officer 387. I am in the area. Please send back-up."

The sun, just rising, drove beams of sunlight into John's eyes as he turned east onto the street. The neighborhood was completely quiet and still. John parked the car and walked up the sidewalk to the home. He rang the bell, looking around cautiously as he waited for someone to open the door. He could hear the sound of a person running down carpeted stairs before the door was flung open and a disheveled woman appeared. "Please, please. You have to help me! He's crazy," she said in a panic.

A man started to descend the stairs behind the woman. John pulled the woman outside and pushed her to the side of the house. "Stay here. Don't move!"

The man on the stairs looked as if he hadn't slept that night; perhaps he hadn't slept in days. His shirt was half-tucked into his pants, and he was barefoot. John saw a glint of metal in the man's hand and took two steps back from the door. He drew his gun, pointed it at the man, and told him to stop. The man continued down two more steps, reaching the main floor, ten feet from where

John stood. It was clear now that the man was holding a knife, a large kitchen knife with a wide blade.

"Stop! Stop! Put the knife down!" John yelled at him. "Stop! Stop! Drop it!" John continued taking small steps backward, away from the man. He had seen videos at the police academy of how quickly someone with a knife could attack and stab a victim. Officers are instructed to use lethal force when confronting a person with a knife, which is considered a truly fatal weapon. Tasers, pepper spray, or other nonlethal means are never appropriate, according to police training, when threatened with a knife.

John, finger resting on the trigger now, was praying not to have to shoot this man. "Put the weapon down! Now! Put it down! Now!"

The man looked John in the eye. He didn't move. John's heart was beating so fast and so hard that it was all he could hear in his head. He was panting out breaths, but trying desperately to stay controlled. He knew how powerful an adrenaline dump could be on the body. First the hearing goes, then comes the tunnel vision, the shortness of breath, and rapid heartbeat. John had been trained at the academy to fight through the effects of such an adrenaline overload, and he worked to overcome the symptoms.

"I will shoot you. Don't do this. Don't do this. You don't want this. Put the knife down." John pleaded with the man standing in the doorway of the house. "You don't want this." John knew that he was dangerously close to the man and would have to shoot him if he made one more move toward him. The man stared at John. John's finger tightened around the trigger, preparing for what he believed to be inevitable.

The man slowly released his grip on the knife, and it fell to the floor. Then he slowly raised his hands into the air. A police car, John's back-up, pulled onto the curb, and another officer ran up with his weapon drawn. "Get down! Get down! Now! On the ground!" the officer commanded as he ran. The man looked at both officers, and slumped to his knees.

〜

Recent studies have shown that 21 to 30 percent of officers suffer from post-traumatic stress disorder (PTSD) (Cortez and Ball; Chopko and Schwartz). Some scholars argue that traumatic events, like the one described in the previous story, lead to psychological stress (Marshall), but others claim that everyday stressors like critical supervisors, challenging coworkers, and micromanagement create the stressful work environment that is law enforcement (Stinchcomb). In all likelihood, it is a combination of both factors that results in police having one of the most stressful of all professions (Burke; Colwell et al.).

I only remember the first day my husband wore a police uniform, not the last. We have never discussed what it was like for him to turn in his gun and badge and walk away. Six years is enough time to reach burnout as a police officer. I didn't know it was the end. I only knew it was miserable. John had started drinking more. We spoke less and less about what happened on his shifts and more and more about his problems with colleagues, the chief, and the department. As he withdrew from work and life, I withdrew from him.

Regarding police burnout, Cortez and Ball report, "Constantly fearing for and worrying about personal safety, the safety of others, and the concern of performing to expectations of others are emotionally draining" (19). The emotional exhaustion John experienced on the job affected our marriage, and I soon suffered from my own emotional overload. When John approached me to tell me he was resigning from the police department, I was empty of compassion. I shrugged my shoulders and said something like, "Whatever you want to do." This response was in sharp contrast to what I had told him years earlier. Before he was even out of the police academy, we had agreed that the minute I saw his behavior or personality change due to police work, I was going to ask him to leave the force. We thought we were really smart to agree so early to be on guard for symptoms of burnout. We acted as if we would somehow magically see the signs of PTSD, depression, and weariness. But we didn't just fortuitously see them and redirect our lives accordingly. It was a long, slow descent into the place where we ended up, strangers with nothing to say to one another. And when it was time to leave the force, it was his decision and not mine.

At one point, John and I kept a tally of the officers who had divorced during his time at the police department. There was a separate tally for those who quit, were fired, or were arrested. Of the eight men and women who graduated in my husband's academy class, only John and one other were still at the same department as police officers six years later. Chopko and Schwartz note that trauma symptoms experienced by police officers, specifically hyper-arousal and greater avoidance, correspond with more assaults being committed by officers when on duty and reduced interest in maintaining personal relationships. Traumatic events that officers encounter on the job end up impacting their job performance and their personal lives. In the article "Bullet Points," Wolfe, a retired police officer and current police academy trainer, argues that his goal for police cadets is to have "positive, healthy, long retirements. The biggest stumbling block to that goal isn't a felon's gun—it is the cumulative effect of the stress of the job on health, both mental and physical."

After my husband resigned, our marriage slowly recovered. As weeks turned into months, John grew less sullen and depressed. We stayed in close contact with only a few officers, primarily the ones who had seen John through his difficult times and had experienced feelings similar to his own. Looking back, I see now how dangerously close we were to losing each other—how dangerously close we were to losing ourselves.

Conclusion

> My personal opinion is, you have a lot of weapons on your belt; most of those you go your whole career and never use, or one percent of the time you might use. The weapons that you use the most—your mouth, your demeanor, your body language, report writing—you train very little in them.
>
> —Sergeant Kevin Chapman, Jackson Police Department

CURIOUS TO DISCOVER THE OUTCOME OF THE DOMESTIC violence dispute that instigated Officer Lewis's report detailed in this book, I contacted the district court clerk in Jackson for information. I found that the man in the case, Michael, pled guilty to the charge of Domestic Battery 3rd Degree. He was assessed fines totaling $260 and was sentenced to three days in jail with credit for time served. Michael may or may not have actually felt he was guilty of Domestic Battery 3rd Degree when he pled. He may have decided not to bother with more court dates or with hiring an attorney. It could also be that his court-appointed attorney advised him to plead rather than fight the case. Whatever the circumstances concerning his decision to plead, he will now have a domestic violence charge on his record.

The woman, Pamela, initially pled not guilty to Domestic Battery 3rd Degree. At her trial, the judge found her guilty of a lesser charge of Disorderly Conduct. She was ordered to pay $240 in fines and was sentenced to one day in jail with credit for time served. The charge of Disorderly Conduct is a much less serious charge than Domestic Battery 3rd Degree, and it is likely that the judge did not have evidence to support the initial charge.

It would be interesting to see how differently Michael's case would have turned out had he done the same as Pamela and pled not guilty. Perhaps at his trial the judge would have made the same determination and lowered his charge to Disorderly Conduct, or perhaps the woman's testimony and that of the officer would have persuaded the judge that Michael had instigated the fight. The reality is that both individuals were ultimately charged with crimes based on the report written by Officer Lewis, and these two people now have criminal records that will follow them for the rest of their lives.

THE VARIED PURPOSES OF A POLICE REPORT

For Officer Lewis, the report's main purpose is as a mnemonic device to help him remember details if he has to testify in court. Secondary to that purpose is an explanation of the probable cause that led to the arrest and the inclusion of the elements of a crime that helped him determine a criminal charge was appropriate. Officer Lewis claims that a good report helps him to CYA, meaning a report's purpose is to keep the supervisor, defense attorney, and others from criticizing his actions or his report writing. The police supervisor mostly agrees with the officer about the report's purpose. He thinks a good report is one that helps the officer's memory. He seems to share Officer Lewis's preoccupation with the court, and wants officers to be protected from a potential defense attorney attack based on poor grammar or content in the report. The notion of appearing professional and presenting the image of a competent officer is very important to both officer and supervisor, and writing a professional-looking report is working toward this aim.

The attorneys interviewed for this study have strikingly different purposes for the report when compared to the officer and supervisor. The prosecutor needs a report to help him determine that the elements of the crime match a criminal charge and that there is sufficient evidence to take the case to trial if necessary. He does not seem to care at all about the professionalism of the document. He wants the report to include everything he needs to know, but at the end of his interview, he admits, "And they should know what I need to know. And, you know, the reality is they don't." The defense attorney, similarly, wants the document to be an a-rhetorical text, objectively listing everything that happened. He wants to be able to sort out what happened on his own, based on the facts provided by the officer. While the defense attorney wants the objective facts, he is also reading the report to look for holes in the document. He uses any holes in evidence to develop a defense and tear down the credibility of the officer. So although he believes a report's purpose should be to objectively detail everything that happened, the defense attorney actually reads the report with the aim of discovering what has been left out.

The judge argues that the report should serve the purposes of the officer and the prosecutor. He wants a document that helps the officer remember what happened because he knows that officers use police reports to help them on the stand during trial. In addition, the judge knows that the prosecutor uses the report to build a case and determine probable cause. But the judge and the defense attorney share many civil rights concerns, and both look to the report to answer important questions about consent, Miranda rights, and searches.

Despite acknowledging in some way that reports must serve all of these purposes, the judge actually shows a great deal of empathy for Officer Lewis concerning the lack of detail and witness information in the report. The judge assumes that the officer is suffering from some form of burnout or apathy and largely excuses the report's shortcomings. The judge may realize consciously or unconsciously that the demands on a police report are incredibly difficult to meet and that some requirements are impossible. Due to time and memory constraints, officers can't possibly offer every detail of an event, especially those they don't see as important at the time. It is also unlikely that in a report, an officer would ever admit to making a mistake, failing to ask for consent, or in some other way neglecting police procedure.

HIGH STAKES FOR REPORT WRITERS AND READERS

Herndl and Licona argue, "The authority to speak . . . is a social identity that is occupied by a concrete individual but emerges from a set of social practices" (142). Police officers need to determine and assert their authority and ethos in their reports. As evidenced by Officer Lewis and his supervisor, Tom Cuddy, a great deal of energy is put into creating a professional ethos for the officer in report writing. At stake for an officer are his or her credibility and authority if the readers in the chained literacy event question the presentation of facts. Even more concerning is the idea that an officer will be "hammered" (to use Officer Lewis's term) on the stand at trial. It is important for officers to avoid language or content that they think will jeopardize their credibility, status, reputation, or authority. The supervisor, likewise, has the department's credibility and authority at stake. Cuddy wants Officer Lewis to produce a good report for court, one that helps Lewis appear knowledgeable and capable as an officer. Lewis's performance of agency in writing reports can have a direct impact on the department's identity as credible and professional. The prosecutor mentions during his interview that he would speak with Lewis's supervisor and "inquire about his level of training," should they both be made to look bad in court. This implies that the supervisor's own reputation and authority are on the line as well.

The prosecutor speaks so passionately about this report in his interview because he realizes what is at stake for him regarding the report. Prosecutors rely on police reports for every charging decision that they make. If information isn't in the report, prosecutors are extremely unlikely to learn about it otherwise. They depend on the report for their own status as "good" prosecutors. Mark Guston, the prosecutor interviewed for this study, was adamant about what the police report should and should not do. He wants a completely objective document that does not advocate for the officer because a report that engages in that kind of advocacy is harmful to the prosecutor's understanding of what actually happened. Guston's reputation is at stake when making charging decisions because, as he puts it, "Now I've got a shitty case on the docket, and all it looks like is the prosecutor is dismissing domestic batteries." It damages his reputation as a prosecutor if he dismisses too many domestic battery cases due to poor reports. He knows that the public won't understand the root cause and will blame him. He will suffer the consequences caused by writers over whom he has very little control or authority.

In addition, Guston is trying to establish his own authority through his interpretation and use of the police report. He complains that officers try to embellish the report, adding, "I don't need extra adjectives. I don't need it. I mean, 'He was upset. She was agitated. She was bleeding.' Not bleeding 'profusely'! Take a picture. I will determine if it was profusely or not." Guston wants to establish the facts and details of the case based on Officer Lewis's objective observations. He does not want the officer displaying the kind of authority Guston feels is reserved for prosecutors.

The defense attorney and the judge admittedly have less at stake than the other readers. A defense attorney's reputation and authority can really only be increased by a poor report, so he has little of the passion that the prosecutor displays regarding the missing elements in the report. For the defense, reports offer information that helps determine how the attorney will proceed with the case. If the report is a good report for the prosecutor, then the defense may decide to have a client plea rather than go to trial. If, however, the report is missing details, witness information, or a logical chronology of events, then the defense attorney has a good shot at trying the case and diminishing the officer's authority and credibility on the stand. This action paradoxically will increase the defense attorney's own authority.

The judge, on the other hand, admits that a good report "does make [his] job a lot easier." He explains that if a report helps an officer's memory, this in turn helps the judicial process at trial. Reports serve the judge by helping witnesses and officers remember details about the events in question. This small memory concern, however, is dwarfed by what is at stake for the judicial process. Though the judge himself might have very little at stake regarding police reports, he acknowledges that the system is greatly impacted by the documents. Police reports can reveal appropriate police practices by stating how civil rights were upheld explicitly. Or reports can hide violations of civil rights by not expressly stating that Miranda was read, consent was given, and so on. The violation of individual rights is a very serious matter that the judge and defense attorney discuss at length in their interviews.

The victims and suspects named in the police report have the most at stake in all of this. Suspects face possible jail time, a criminal record, time away from family, the loss of income, and a new identity as a "criminal." Similarly, the victims named in a police report rely on the power of the document to bring them justice, safety, retribution, and peace. The stakes are very high indeed for both groups, and yet they have very little say in how the police report will be written and what its impact will be in the legal system. The Jackson police chief, Stephen Mathes, stated in our interview,

> A mistake in content in reports can really hurt an officer. You will truly lose a case in court, and let me tell you the problem with that. Losing a case should be significant to an officer, not because you lose, but because some victim has been victimized again by the system. By your poor-quality work, a victim was victimized again.

Almost all of us in composition and rhetoric, and in technical writing, teach one form or another of the report genre. It is important for our students to understand the people and institutions impacted by their writing. We need to teach audience and purpose when we teach specific genres, but we also need to discuss how documents are used, how they accrue power for writers and readers, and how these documents are used for ideological purposes as well. It is not enough to offer students a description of audience—age, education, socioeconomic class, reading ability, and so on. Students must understand that readers can change the reading for their own purposes and uphold or diminish the power of the writer and document. Especially in the case of readers with more cultural and social capital, documents that were written for one purpose can be manipulated to serve another, sometimes contradictory, purpose. Writers occupy positions of authority when writing in various genres, and our students need to understand the position they take when acting as agents.

THE CIRCULATION OF POWER IN
THE CHAINED LITERACY EVENT

In this text I have used Bourdieu's descriptions of cultural capital (knowledge, competency); social capital (status, reputation); and symbolic capital (the control or power that people, organizations, or systems exert over their environments and over others) to describe the types of power that circulate in the police report genre ("The Forms" 241–58; "Social Space" 17–24). From the writer to each reader, these categories of capital are bestowed, contested, or depleted at each link in the chained literacy event. The audience for the report determines whether the writer has authority and various types of capital and power.

At nearly every stage of the chained literacy event, the cultural and social capital of the writer and reader are at stake. In writing the document, an officer is trying to increase his or her own social capital by establishing his or her cultural capital and ethos. If successful, this capital can transfer to the supervisor and ultimately the department. The police report accrues power if the supervisor agrees that it is a good report and forwards it on to the next link in the chain. The increase in social and cultural capital at this stage can result in symbolic power for the police department members as agents of the institution who work to create documents that circulate power back to the department. The more police reports that are determined to be "good" by readers higher in the hierarchal chain, the more social capital the department earns.

However, reports that are written to advocate for an officer's actions, a form of defense or argument in the presentation of evidence, damage officer ethos and further solidify the need for a report to be questioned. Although officers think they are increasing their cultural and social capital by advocating for their actions in reports, these forms of capital are actually diminished. This affects the police department as well. When readers question the credibility and authority of one officer, the social capital of the entire department can be depleted. Readers will question how this officer was trained, how such a report got through the department, and whether poor reports are standard at this police department.

The prosecutor and defense attorney have a paradoxical relationship to the police report genre and its power. The knowledge created in the police report is vital for the prosecutor's office. A prosecutor needs to know and understand what happened via the police report so the right charge can be filed and justice can be served. A good report helps the prosecutorial office do its job and raises its cultural capital. If the prosecutor's office is able to utilize several good reports, then its overall social capital and standing in the community can be elevated. A poor report hurts the prosecutor's cultural and social capital. Guston stated in his interview that a bad report could make him "look like a dumbass." He has very little control over how reports are written, yet police reports have a significant impact on the office of the prosecutor and his or her standing in the community. On the other hand, defense attorneys may enjoy an increase in social capital when reports are poor. The mistakes and holes left in a police report by an officer are issues that a defense attorney can capitalize on when building a defense for the client. The more the defense attorney can attack an officer's credibility and authority, the more cultural and social capital can be obtained for the attorney and the client. Of course, when this happens, the officer, supervisor, and prosecutor lose cultural and social capital.

A judge has a great deal of cultural, social, and symbolic capital due to his or her position, education, and experience as a lawyer prior to becoming a judge. It seems to me that it is difficult to impact this capital via the police report. Although Judge Laffoon mentions that a good report can make his job easier, I don't think a good report can make him more powerful. A good report serves the officer, the department, and the State, in the judge's opinion. A poor report does not really accrue power for the position of judge (unlike the defense attorney) because the judge is merely overseeing the case and determining through testimony what circumstances and evidence are relevant in the case. In terms of symbolic capital, though, Judge Laffoon has lots of questions about the civil rights and consents afforded in the report he reviewed for this study.

If police officers regularly leave out important individual rights concerns, a judge has difficulty determining if proper legal procedures were followed. Considering the current public outrage toward law enforcement's perceived cover-ups and systemic racism concerns, it is vital that constitutional rights are plainly discussed in police reports. The lack of such transparency damages the symbolic capital of the legal system, especially for police officers and departments.

Academic papers, letters to the editor, dissertations, police reports, news articles, Internet blogs, and all other genres are sites where the readers determine the ethos, power, and effectiveness of the writing itself. Students need to see themselves as occupying spaces of power when they write, and understand how these positions can be manipulated and changed by readers. Conversely, as readers, students should be made aware of their power to determine rhetorical effectiveness and ethos of writers. They should be introduced to the larger power structures in which we all write and produce documents.

THE POLICE REPORT GENRE IN THE LEGAL SYSTEM

Police officers and police departments own the police report genre and are ultimately responsible for its creation and practice, though the State (prosecutor and others) can have an important impact on the way reports are written and used in the legal system. The creation and maintenance of the genre reveals the ideology of the group that replicates and reinforces it. Devitt asserts that genres reflect "a group's values, epistemology, and power relationships—its ideology" (*Writing* 60). Competing values and ideologies are at the heart of the police report genre.

The first conflict occurs before the police report has even left the police department. While supervisors request an emotionless, affect-free report, they often also request officers to write a police report like a story. I have heard the phrase "paint the picture" hundreds of times while interviewing officers and others about the report-writing process. Officer Lewis used it in our interview to describe his intention in writing the report. I have also heard this phrase during police academy classes and from police trainers. "Paint the picture" is meant to imply that officers should think of every incident as a story and write it so that the reader has a complete sense of what occurred. Kevin Chapman, a Jackson police supervisor, notes, "I like it [the report] to be written like a story, and I will tell you why. We are very myopic in our views about who reads these things and who matters, who can understand." Police value narrative, but only narrative devoid of affect and any multilingual markers. "Uniform" Standard English does not have room for ethnic or language diversity. The white masculine rhetoric of the report demands only the who, what, when, where, how, and why, but officers are asked to write a story at the same time, a nonwhite rhetoric.

In the interviews I conducted, the prosecutor and defense attorney want objective observations with no conclusions or summary in the report. They don't want a story. Or, maybe they do. The difference is that both the officer and the attorneys want to create their own narratives. The officer wants to create his narrative out of the events he observed, while the prosecutor and defense attorney want to create their own narratives based on the observations of the event, unaltered by the opinions of the officer.

The relationship of the police report genre to power is complicated in such a multifaceted environment where officers' writing is constantly questioned. In such positions, officers may feel the need to defend themselves and their actions, effectively writing a defense into every police report. The genre, then, has become a rhetorical genre designed to aid in the creation of police officers' and departments' cultural and social capital. This development in the genre came about as officers and departments were disciplined by the system for creating reports that didn't serve the State; however, this disciplining hasn't created better reports. It has, in effect, created documents that can remain silent about significant details rather than expose them and leave the writer vulnerable.

It is important for us and for our students to understand how genres operate in powerful institutions. Blythe argues, "Many of our graduates, regardless of their major . . . will produce the texts

that play a part in maintaining an organization" (168). We can pre-
pare students for these environments by helping them think critically about the role that written texts play in an organization and
the complicity they have in recreating the institution through documents. When students understand the role that employees play in
supporting powerful systems, they can better decide what role they
want to play or how they might change that role, versus blindly following the dictates of the genre and the system. Blythe argues that
"being able to 'read' an organization involves a type of literacy—a
type of literacy to which we should attend" (168). Teaching our
students to read institutions empowers them to decide what role
they will play in supporting or deconstructing those institutions. In
their academic and other careers, they will be able to discern ideologies and power that were previously invisible to them.

THE FUTURE OF POLICE REPORT WRITING

Following a wave of court cases and investigations into police racially
profiling citizens in the late 1990s, police departments around the
country began outfitting police cars with cameras (Westphal). Currently, a majority of patrol cars in the United States are equipped
with onboard cameras (Reaves 3). Though officers may have initially disliked the cameras, they soon realized they could use the
video to help them remember details for their written reports. In
addition, video could now clear officers of false citizen complaints
and validate the use of force if incidents were caught on film (Westphal). Despite the welcomed advantages of onboard video cameras,
police reports have not improved in the ways that prosecutors and
judges would like. Some officers admit that because they rely on
the video to aid their report writing, their investigation and note-
taking skills have actually declined (Westphal). So while technology
has helped officers do their jobs more effectively and has helped departments track vehicle stops for racial profiling, it has not helped
improve the practice of report writing.

Similar to the call for more technology in the 1990s, recent examples of police brutality and shootings have prompted many to
call for the use of body cameras on police officers. Body cameras

differ from in-car cameras because they are worn by individual officers and record everything an officer says and does outside of the vehicle. President Obama created a proposal after the shooting death
of Michael Brown in Ferguson, Missouri, in order to dramatically
increase the number of body cameras in police departments around
the country (Ehrenfreund). In 2015, the US Justice Department
awarded more than $23 million to seventy-three agencies in thirty-
two states for body camera purchases and training (Department of
Justice, Office of Public Affairs). Body cameras should help departments and communities alike understand what happened in events
like Michael Brown's death and others. However, I don't think that
the adoption of these devices is likely to improve report writing any
more than in-car video cameras did two decades ago.

I do think there is hope, though, for police reports, and I think
police report training could serve as a vehicle to discuss and approach the issues within the genre. Villanueva argues, "Our assumptions about how the world works are influenced by—might
even be created by—the language we receive and use. Large things.
World views. Now, if that's the case, then we're also affected by the
language we don't use" (5). It is critical that officers speak about
and are trained to think about racism, implicit bias, and stereotypes
and the ways in which biases impact their decisions. In addition,
officers would benefit from learning about the ways in which we
discuss writing in our field. Discussions centered on rhetoric, audience awareness, agency, and power could help officers see the work
that their writing does within the justice system. I also think it is
paramount that prosecutors engage in formal and informal conversations with officers at police departments and participate in training new officers at the police academy. Both the prosecutor's office
and the police department would benefit from such an exchange of
ideas and knowledge.

In terms of other new training for officers, rhetorical listening
could prove to be a particularly powerful and effective practice to
share with police officers and others in law enforcement. Ratcliffe
claims that "*rhetorical listening* signifies a stance of openness that a
person may choose to assume in relation to *any* person, text, or cul-

ture" (17). She asks teachers to challenge their students to make the following moves, but I would extend that request to police trainers and all officers: "to recognize how *all* our lives are implicated within cultural diversity; to acknowledge that we *all* possess a responsibility for naming, explaining, and addressing these implications; and to understand the categories of *dominant, nondominant,* and even *mythical norm* are socially constructed and fluid, changing over time and place, in ways that influence *all* our lives" (136). Rhetorical listening could aid officers in overcoming implicit bias. It could also help officers begin to analyze and understand the nature of the police report genre and the way in which victims are served (or not served) by police documents. It is impossible, at this point, to eliminate all of the conflicts and contradictions of the police report genre itself, but enhanced training, combined with new practices focused on rhetorical listening and community building, offer hope.

NOTES

Introduction

1. Walter Scott was fatally shot by a police officer on April 4, 2015. The police officer, Michael Slager, was arrested and charged with murder. According to video evidence and reports, Walter Scott was unarmed and running away from Officer Slager when he was shot by the officer eight times in the back (Fernandez).
2. Michel Foucault, Karl Marx, and Pierre Bourdieu are perhaps some of the most famous to critique the power of the State.
3. Jackson Police Department is a pseudonym designed to protect the identity of officers I interviewed.
4. I use Barney G. Glasser's grounded theory approach in my research and in this text. In *Theoretical Sensitivity* he writes, "The goal of grounded theory is to generate a conceptual theory that accounts for a pattern of behavior which is relevant and problematic for those involved. The goal is not voluminous description, nor clever verification" (93). In later publications, Glasser notes that grounded theory mandates the researcher "to remain open to what is actually happening and not to start filtering data through pre-conceived hypotheses and biases to listen and observe and thereby discover the main concern of the participants in the field and how they resolve this concern" (Glasser and Holton 57).
5. The name Jackson, Arkansas, is an alias designed to protect the identity of research participants. Population demographics (using the actual city name) were obtained from city-data.com.
6. Information was obtained from censusviewer.com.
7. See Clay Spinuzzi's book *Tracing Genres through Organizations* for methodology designed to study genres in organizations.

Micro-Chapter: The Fire

1. These terms were first used by Kenneth Pike and described in his book *Language in Relation to a Unified Theory of the Structure of*

Human Behavior, but were quickly adapted for use by ethnographers working in the field of anthropology. Marvin Harris, one of the first to do so, utilized the descriptions of etic and emic to describe the various ways anthropologic researchers might define language in use. I most closely align my understanding of the terms to the way they are now used in ethnographic research. Harry Wolcott describes the emic approach as the "insider" view, while the etic is the "outsider" (144). He also explains that today's ethnographers do a bit of both, and that the category of insider or outsider is not as clearly defined as it once was.

1. Writing for Institutional Memory and Self-Preservation

1. See Seawright's vignette "Night Blind: The Places of Police Writing" in *College Composition and Communication*, Sept. 2014.

2. I utilized descriptive observation, verbal-probing interview, and discourse-based interview techniques for this study. All interviews were recorded and transcribed. Participants signed IRB-approved release forms and were instructed that their answers were strictly voluntary. I decided against using the thinking-aloud protocol (Flower and Hayes) for my interview with the police officer. I felt the technique would be too intrusive to use with a police officer writing a report. My strategies were derived in part from Odell and Goswami's instructions to social workers in "Writing in a Non-Academic Setting." I also wanted to follow the advice of Lauer and Asher, who support the idea that "researchers do not deliberately structure or control the environment from which the data are gathered" (15). I tried to keep in mind that this officer was on duty and was not at his leisure to discuss his report-writing process for hours at a time. This officer needed to get back on the street, and I needed to try to understand as much as I could as quickly as I could about him as the writer and a reader of this report. For these reasons, I used the cognitive interviewing verbal-probing technique. In this style, "the interviewer asks the target question and the subject answers it, but the interviewer then follows up (either immediately or at the end of the interview) by probing for other specific information relevant to the question or to the specific answer given" (Willis 47). This allowed me to focus our discussion of the report on the audience, and to probe further when the officer responded in a surprising way. In addition, the technique allowed me to ask specific questions about the officer's word and stylistic choices in the report.

3. I have made no changes or corrections, grammatical or otherwise, in the police report narrative. The report was obtained from the Jackson Police Department through the Freedom of Information Act. Names and addresses have been changed in order to protect identities.

2. The Creation and Circulation of Cultural and Social Capital

1. This policy changed during the time I was researching the department. When I first started riding with officers, they had up to a week to turn in reports from the day of the arrest or incident. This allowed them to sleep, consult with other officers, track down evidence or witnesses, and find dedicated writing time during the week to write reports. After the change, officers had to write all their reports at the ends of their shifts. On busy days of the week or during busy shifts, this might mean writing as many as five or six reports in a very short time at the end of an exhausting shift.

3. Authority, Agency, and the Places of Contested Power

1. Unlike Officer Lewis, whom I did not know prior to my ride-along, and Sergeant Cuddy, whom I knew only vaguely, Mark Guston was a close acquaintance. He and my husband were friends for a year prior to my interview with him. I did not coach him in any way for the interview. His passionate responses are typical of his demeanor.

4. Police Reporting and Public Trust

1. Chris Allen and I had met at various times over the course of two or three years. We had friends in the same circles. Although not as familiar to me as Mark Guston, Chris Allen was generous with his time and responses to interview requests.
2. Officers may also be leery of eyewitness testimony because they realize how weak such testimony can actually be. See Elizabeth Loftus's book *Eyewitness Testimony* for more information on the fallibility of eyewitness recollections.

5. Police Procedure, the Legal System, and Circulations of Power

1. In 1966 the Supreme Court in *Miranda v. Arizona* ruled, "The prosecution may not use statements, whether exculpatory or inculpatory, stemming from questioning initiated by law enforcement officers after a person has been taken into custody or otherwise deprived of his freedom of action in any significant way" (Miranda).

In addition, the case stipulated that an individual in State custody must be informed "that he has the right to remain silent, and that anything he says will be used against him in court; he must be clearly informed that he has the right to consult with a lawyer and to have the lawyer with him" (Miranda). All suspects must be read these rights and understand them before being questioned.

2. If they are not free to leave, then the officer must read them their Miranda rights.

WORKS CITED

Bawarshi, Anis. "The Genre Function." *College English* 62.3 (2000): 335–60. Print.

Bazerman, Charles. *Shaping Written Knowledge: The Genre and Activity of the Experimental Article in Science.* Madison: U of Wisconsin P, 1988. Print.

Belfiore, Mary Ellen, Tracy A. Defoe, Sue Folinsbee, Judy Hunter, and Nancy S. Jackson. *Reading Work.* Mahwah: Lawrence Erlbaum, 2004. Print.

Bivens v. Six Unknown Named Agents of Fed. Bureau of Narcotics. 403 USA 388 No 301. Supreme Court of the US. 21 June 1971. *FindLaw for Legal Professionals.* FindLaw, n.d. Web. 21 Apr. 2017. <http://case law.findlaw.com/us-supreme-court/403/388.html>.

Blythe, Stuart. "Agencies, Ecologies, and the Mundane Artifacts in Our Midst." *Labor, Writing Technologies, and the Shaping of Composition in the Academy.* Ed. Pamela Takayoshi and Patricia Sullivan. Cresskill: Hampton Press, 2007. 167–86. Print.

Bonilla-Silva, Eduardo. *Racism without Racists: Color-Blind Racism and the Persistence of Racial Inequality in America.* Lanham: Rowman and Littlefield, 2014. Print.

Bourdieu, Pierre. "The Forms of Capital." *Handbook of Theory and Research for the Sociology of Education.* Ed. J. Richardson. Westport: Greenwood Press, 1986. 241–58. Print.

———. *Language and Symbolic Power.* Ed. John B. Thompson. Trans. Gino Raymond and Matthew Adamson. Cambridge: Polity Press, 1991. Print.

———. "Social Space and Symbolic Power." *Sociological Theory* 71.1 (1989): 14–25. Print.

Brand, Alice G. "The Why of Cognition: Emotion and the Writing Process." *College Composition and Communication* 38.4 (1987): 436–43. Print.

Brandt, Deborah. *The Rise of Writing: Redefining Mass Literacy*. Cambridge: Cambridge UP, 2015. Print.

———. "When People Write for Pay." *JAC* 2nd ser. 29.1/2 (2009): 165–97. Print.

Burke, Ronald J. "Stressful Events, Work-Family Conflict, Coping, Psychological Burnout, and Well-Being among Police Officers." *Psychological Reports* 75.2 (1994): 787–800. Print.

Campbell, Elaine. "Police Narrativity in the Risk Society." *British Journal of Criminology* 44.5 (2004): 695–714. Print.

Chopko, Brian A., and Robert C. Schwartz. "Correlates of Career Traumatization and Symptomatology among Active-Duty Police Officers." *Criminal Justice Studies* 25.1 (2012): 83–95. Print.

Clark, Kimberly. *How to Really Really Write Those Boring Police Reports*. New York: Looseleaf Law Publications, 2010. Print.

Colwell, Lori H., Phillip M. Lyons, A. Jerry Bruce, Randall L. Garner, and Rowland S. Miller. "Police Officers' Cognitive Appraisals for Traumatic Events: Implications for Treatment and Training." *Applied Psychology in Criminal Justice* 7.2 (2011): 106–32. Print.

Cortez, Marybel, and Jeremy D. Ball. "Direct v. Indirect Exposure to Trauma: An Insight to Officer Coping Mechanisms." *McNair Scholars Research Journal* 10.1 (2014): 17–28. Print.

Cotugno, Marianne, and Mark Hoffman. "Seeking a Direct Pipeline to Practice: Four Guidelines for Researchers and Practitioners." *Journal of Business and Technical Communication* 25.1 (2011): 95–105. Print.

Davis, Julie Hirschfeld, and Matt Apuzzo. "President Obama Condemns Both the Baltimore Riots and the Nation's 'Slow-Rolling Crisis.'" *Nytimes.com*. New York Times Co., 28 Apr. 2015. Web. 12 May 2015.

Department of Justice. *Department of Justice Report Regarding the Criminal Investigation into the Shooting Death of Michael Brown by Ferguson, Missouri Police Officer Darren Wilson*. *Washingtonpost.com*. Washington Post, 4 Mar. 2015. Web. 17 Mar. 2017. <https://apps.washingtonpost.com/g/documents/national/department-of-justice-report-on-the-michael-brown-shooting/1436/>.

Department of Justice. Office of Public Affairs. "Justice Department Awards over $23 Million in Funding for Body Worn Camera Pilot Program to Support Law Enforcement Agencies in 32 States." *United States Department of Justice*. US Department of Justice, 21 Sept. 2015. Web. 14 Apr. 2017.

Devitt, Amy J. "Generalizing about Genre: New Conceptions of an Old Concept." *College Composition and Communication* 44.4 (1993): 573–86. Print.

————. *Writing Genres.* Carbondale: Southern Illinois UP, 2004. Print.

Devitt, Amy, Anis Bawarshi, and Mary Jo Reiff. "Materiality and Genre in the Study of Discourse Communities." *College English* 65.5 (2003): 541–58. Print.

Ede, Lisa, and Andrea Lunsford. "Among the Audience: On Audience in an Age of New Literacies." *Engaging Audience: Writing in an Age of New Literacies.* Ed. M. Elizabeth Weiser, Brian M. Fehler, and Angela M. Gonzalez. Urbana: NCTE, 2009. 42–69. Print.

————. "Audience Addressed/Audience Invoked: The Role of Audience in Composition Theory and Pedagogy." *College Composition and Communication* 35.2 (1984): 155–71. Print.

Edwards, Derek. "Facts, Norms and Dispositions: Practical Uses of the Modal Verb *Would* in Police Interrogations." *Discourse Studies* 8.4 (2006): 475–501. Print.

Ehrenfreund, Max. "Body Cameras for Cops Could Be the Biggest Change to Come out of the Ferguson Protests." *Washingtonpost.com.* Washington Post, 2 Dec. 2014. Web. 17 Mar. 2017.

Fernandez, Manny. "After Walter Scott Shooting, Scrutiny Turns to 2nd Officer." *Nytimes.com.* New York Times Co., 17 Apr. 2015. Web. 5 May 2015.

Flower, Linda, and John R. Hayes. "A Cognitive Process Theory of Writing." *College Composition and Communication* 32.4 (1981): 365–87. Print.

Foucault, Michel. "The Discourse on Language." *The Continental Philosophy Reader.* Ed. Richard Kearney and Mara Rainwater. New York: Rutledge, 1996. 339–60. Print.

Frankenberg, Ruth. *White Women, Race Matters: The Social Construction of Whiteness.* Minneapolis: U of Minnesota P, 1993. Print.

Frazee, Barbara, and Joseph N. Davis. *Painless Police Report Writing: An English Guide for Criminal Justice Professionals.* Upper Saddle River: Pearson Prentice Hall, 2008. Print.

Giddens, Anthony. *The Constitution of Society: Outline of the Theory of Structuration.* Berkeley: U of California P, 1984.

Glasser, Barney G. *Theoretical Sensitivity: Advances in the Methodology of Grounded Theory.* Mill Valley: Sociology Press, 1978. Print.

Glasser, Barney G., and Judith Holton. "Remodeling Grounded Theory." *Historical Social Research,* Supp. 19 (2007): 47–68.

Hall, Daniel E., Lois A. Ventura, Yung H. Lee, and Eric Lambert. "Suing Cops and Corrections Officers: Officer Attitudes and Experiences about Civil Liability." *Policing* 26.4 (2003): 529–47. Print.

Harris, Marvin. "History and Significance of the Emic/Etic Distinction." *Annual Review of Anthropology* 5 (1976): 329–50. Print.

Haworth, Kate. "The Dynamics of Power and Resistance in Police Interview Discourse." *Discourse & Society* 17.6 (2006): 739–59. Print.

Heath, Shirley Brice. *Ways with Words: Language, Life, and Work in Communities and Classrooms.* Cambridge: Cambridge UP, 1983. Print.

Herndl, Carl G., and Adela C. Licona. "Shifting Agency: Agency, Kairos, and the Possibilities of Social Action." *Communicative Practices in Workplaces and the Professions: Cultural Perspectives on the Regulation of Discourse and Organizations.* Ed. Mark Zachery and Charlotte Thralls. Inverness: Baywood, 2007. 133–54. Print.

Kahneman, Daniel. *Thinking, Fast and Slow.* New York: Farrar, Straus and Giroux, 2011. Print.

Kidwell, Mardi, and Esther Martinez. "'Let Me Tell You about Myself': A Method for Suppressing Subject Talk in a 'Soft Accusation' Interrogation." *Discourse Studies* 12.1 (2010): 65–89. Print.

Komter, Martha. "The Career of a Suspect's Statement: Talk, Text, Context." *Discourse Studies* 14.6 (2012): 731–52. Print.

LA Times Staff. "The L.A. Riots: 24 Years Later." *Timelines.latimes.com.* Los Angeles Times, 26 Apr. 2016. Web. 17 Mar. 2017.

Lauer, Janice M., and J. William Asher. *Composition Research: Empirical Designs.* New York: Oxford UP, 1988. Print.

Lipsitz, George. *The Possessive Investment in Whiteness: How White People Profit from Identity Politics.* Philadelphia: Temple UP, 2006. Print.

Loftus, Elizabeth. *Eyewitness Testimony.* Cambridge: Harvard UP, 1996. Print.

Marshall, Ellen. "Cumulative Career Traumatic Stress (CCTS): A Pilot Study of Traumatic Stress in Law Enforcement." *Journal of Police and Criminal Psychology* 21.1 (2006): 62–71. Print.

Meier, Nicholas, and R. J. Adams. *Plain English for Cops.* Durham: Carolina Academic Press, 1999. Print.

Michael, A. S. *The Best Police Report Writing Book with Samples: Written for Police by Police, This Is Not an English Lesson.* Charleston: CreateSpace, 2009. Print.

Miller, Carolyn. "Genre as Social Action." *Quarterly Journal of Speech* 70.2 (1984): 151–67. Print.

Miller, Myron, and Paula Pomerenke. "Police Reports Must Be Reader Based." *Law and Order* 37.9 (1989): 66–69. Print.

Mills, Charles W. *The Racial Contract.* Ithaca: Cornell UP, 1997. Print.

Miranda v. Arizona. 484 US 436 No. 759. Supreme Court of the US. 13 June 1966. *FindLaw for Legal Professionals.* FindLaw, n.d. Web. 21

Apr. 2017. <http://caselaw.findlaw.com/us-supreme-court/384/436.
html>.

Odell, Lee, and Dixie Goswami, "Writing in a Non-Academic Setting."
Research in the Teaching of English 16.3 (1982): 201–23. Print.

Ornatowski, Cezar M. "Between Efficiency and Politics: Rhetoric and
Ethics in Technical Writing." *Readings for Technical Communication.*
Ed. Jennifer McLennan. New York: Oxford UP, 2007. 311–19. Print.

Paré, Anthony. "Genre and Identity: Individuals, Institutions, and Ide-
ology." *Relations, Locations, Positions: Composition Theory for Writing
Teachers.* Ed. Peter Vandenberg, Sue Hum, and Jennifer Clary-Lemon.
Urbana: NCTE, 2006. 138–56. Print.

Pike, Kenneth. *Language in Relation to a Unified Theory of the Structures of
Human Behavior.* 2nd ed. The Hague: Mouton, 1967. Print.

Ratcliffe, Krista. *Rhetorical Listening: Identification, Gender, Whiteness.*
Carbondale: Southern Illinois UP, 2006. Print.

Reaves, Brian A. "Local Police Departments, 2013: Equipment and
Technology." US Department of Justice. Bureau of Justice Statistics.
NCJ248767. July 7, 2015. Web. 14 Apr. 2017. <http://www.bjs.gov/
index.cfm?ty=pbdetail&iid=5321>.

Rock, Frances. "The Genesis of a Witness Statement." *International Journal of Speech, Language and the Law* 8.2 (2001): 44–72. Print.

Seawright, Leslie. "Night Blind: The Places of Police Writing." *College
Composition and Communication* 66.1 (2014): 18–20. Print.

Spinuzzi, Clay. *Tracing Genres through Organizations: A Sociocultural Approach to Information Design.* Cambridge: MIT P, 2003. Print.

Stinchcomb, Jeanne B. "Searching for Stress in all the Wrong Places:
Combating Chronic Organizational Stressors in Policing." *Police Practice and Research* 5.3 (2004): 259–77. Print.

Stokoe, Elizabeth, and Derek Edwards. "'Black This, Black That': Racial
Insults and Reported Speech in Neighbour Complaints and Police Interrogations." *Discourse & Society* 18.3 (2007): 337–72. Print.

Strassmann, Mark. "Florida Looks to Expand Controversial Stand Your
Ground Law." *CBS News.com.* CBS, 10 Mar. 2014. Web. 17 Mar.
2017.

Villanueva, Victor. "Blind: Talking about the New Racism." *Writing Center Journal* 26.1 (2006): 3–19. Print.

Westphal, Lonnie. "The In-Car Camera: Value and Impact." *policechief-
magazine.org.* International Association of Chiefs of Police, Aug. 2004.
Web. 17 Mar. 2017.

Willis, Gordon B. *Cognitive Interviewing: A Tool for Improving Question-
naire Design.* Thousand Oaks: Sage, 2005. Print.

Winsor, Dorothy A. *Writing Power: Communication in an Engineering Center*. Albany: State U of New York, 2003. Print.

Winter, Tim. "Michael Brown Shooting: Why Ferguson Police Never Filed an 'Incident Report.'" *NBCnews.com*. NBC, 22 Aug. 2014. Web. 26 May 2015.

Wolcott, Harry F. *Ethnography: A Way of Seeing*. 2nd ed. Lanham: AltaMira Press, 2008. Print.

Wolfe, Duane. "Prioritizing Mental and Physical Health." Excerpt. "Bullet Points: Challenges Facing Police Trainers in 2014." *Policeone.com*. PoliceOne.com, 14 Jan. 2014. Web. 26 May 2015.

INDEX

116 / Index

cameras, 101–2
Campbell, Elaine, xi
capital. *See* cultural capital; social
    capital; symbolic capital
chained literacy events, xvii–xix, 42,
    97–99
chain of command, xvii
Chopko, Brian A., 89, 90
city attorney's office, 37–38
civil liability, 11–12, 79
civil liberties and civil rights
    defense attorneys and concern with,
        59–62
    Miranda rights, 78–79
    race and civil rights laws, xxii
Clark, Kimberly, xii
"color-blindness," claim of, xxii–xxiii
Colwell, Lori H., 89
consent, 60–62
Constitution, US, 60–61
constrained agency, 10
Cortez, Marybel, 89
Cotugno, Marianne, xi
courts and trials
    cross-examination, 16, 18, 29, 71
    jury members as audience, 28
    officer perceptions of, 8
    suppression hearings, 53, 55–57, 72
    See also defense attorneys as readers;
        judges as readers; prosecutors as
        readers
cross-examination
    likelihood of future court
        appearance by officer, 18
    officer fears of, 16, 18, 71
    supervisor views, 29
cultural capital
    circulation of power and, 97–99
    competition for, 10
    concept of, xxiv
    defense attorneys and, 63, 72, 98
    department and, 33
    judges and, 84, 98–99
    knowledge creation by reports and,
        77

mnemonics and, 84
prosecutors and, 40, 41–44, 53, 98
report-writing and, 21
supervisors and, 29, 33
custodial interrogation, 78

Davis, Joseph N., xii
Davis, Julie Hirschfeld, xxi
decision making as inherent in report
    writing, 50–51
defense attorneys as readers
    building the defense, 71–73
    consent and civil liberties concerns,
        59–62
    failures of officer advocacy and
        nearly impossible demands of the
        genre, 68–70
    in hierarchical chain of readers, xviii
    narrative and, 100
    officer views of, 18
    representation and authority in
        reports and, 62–64
    role of, xix
    rules of discovery and, 44–45
    stakes for, 95
    suppression hearings and, 53,
        55–57, 72
    WYSIATI and police reports as
        rhetorical documents, 65–67
Devitt, Amy J., xx, 36, 50, 71, 74,
    86, 99
discipline, 11, 71
discovery, rules of, 44–49

economic capital, 34
Ede, Lisa, xiv–xv
education levels of officers, 29–30
Edwards, Derek, xi
Ehrenfreund, Max, 102
"emic approach," 106n
"etic approach," 106n
evidence
    clear and properly linked, 47
    consent and Fourth Amendment
        rights, 60–62

judicial, 79
proper procedure and, 83
silencing of certain speakers, 64
See also agency
probable cause, 28–29, 48, 60, 66,
77, 83
professionalization, 30, 33–36
prosecutors as readers
adjectives and interpretation vs.
facts and, 48–49
agency, readers, the report genre,
and, 49–51
authority and cultural/social capital,
39–44, 53
circulation of power and, 98
city attorney's office and, 37–38
conversational evidence and, 62–63
in hierarchical chain of readers, xviii
narrative and, 100
officers justifying their actions and,
48, 53
officer views of, 18, 19–20
purpose and instrumental value,
issue of, 51–53
resources spent filling in missing
information, 53
role of, xix
rules of discovery and information
constraints on, 44–49
stakes for, 94–95
subpoenas and, 76
supervisor views of, 27, 28–29
public criticism and scrutiny,
institutional insecurity from, 34
purpose, 51–53, 92–93

race and racism, xv, xxi–xxiii, 29–30
Ratcliffe, Krista, xxii–xxiii, 102–3
rarefaction, 63
reading of police reports. *See specific
types of readers*
Reaves, Brian A., 101
Reiff, Mary Jo, 50, 71
revisions to police reports, 9–10,
31–33

rhetorical documents, police reports
as, 65–67, 100
rhetorical listening, 102–3
rhetorical savvy vs. objectivity, 70
Rice, Tamir, xxi
Rock, Frances, xi

Schwartz, Robert C., 89, 90
Scott, Walter, xi, xxi, 105n
searches and seizures, unreasonable,
60–61
Seawright, Leslie, 106n
silencing of certain speakers, 63–64
Slager, Michael, 105n
social capital
circulation of power and, 97–99
competition for, 10
concept of, xxiv
defense attorneys and, 63, 98
judges and, 84, 98–99
prosecutors and, 41–44, 53, 98
report-writing, officer competency,
and, 8, 20, 21
supervisors and, 29
social fields, 10
Spinuzzi, Clay, 105n
stakes for writers and readers, 93–96
Stinchcomb, Jeanne B., 89
Stokoe, Elizabeth, xi
Strassmann, Mark, xxii
stress, 89–90
subjectivity. *See objectivity vs.
subjectivity*
subpoenas, 75–76
supervisors as readers
as first readers, 26
in hierarchical chain of readers,
xvii–xviii
looking for basics and readability,
27–29
officer views of, 18–19
professionalization, capital, and,
33–36
revision requests and
"micromanaging," 31–33

AUTHOR

Leslie Seawright is associate professor of English at Missouri State University. Seawright's research interests include workplace communication, community literacy practices, technical writing, intercultural communication, and transnational education. She is the editor of two books on transnational education and the author of several articles and book chapters related to police writing, technical communication, and technical writing pedagogy.

BOOKS IN THE CCCC STUDIES IN WRITING & RHETORIC SERIES

This book was typeset in Garamond and Frutiger by Barbara Frazier.
Typefaces used on the cover include Adobe Garamond and Formata.
The book was printed on 55-lb. Natural Offset paper
by King Printing Company, Inc.